CHINA, JAPAN, AND THE U.S.A.

CHINA, JAPAN, AND THE U.S.A.

PRESENT-DAY CONDITIONS IN THE FAR EAST AND THEIR BEARING ON THE WASHINGTON CONFERENCE

JOHN DEWEY

WILDSIDE PRESS

CHINA, JAPAN, AND THE U.S.A.

Published by Wildside Press LLC.

INTRODUCTORY NOTE

The articles following are reprinted as they were written in spite of the fact that any picture of contemporary events is modified by subsequent increase of knowledge and by later events. In the main, however, the writer would still stand by what was said at the time. A few foot notes have been inserted where the text is likely to give rise to misapprehensions. The date of writing has been retained as a guide to the reader.

I

ON TWO SIDES OF THE EASTERN SEAS

It is three days' easy journey from Japan to China. It is doubtful whether anywhere in the world another journey of the same length brings with it such a complete change of political temper and belief. Certainly it is greater than the alteration perceived in journeying directly from San Francisco to Shanghai. The difference is not one in customs and modes of life; that goes without saying. It concerns the ideas, beliefs and alleged information current about one and the same fact: the status of Japan in the international world and especially its attitude toward China. One finds everywhere in Japan a feeling of uncertainty, hesitation, even of weakness. There is a subtle nervous tension in the atmosphere as of a country on the verge of change but not knowing where the change will take it. Liberalism is in the air, but genuine liberals are encompassed with all sorts of difficulties especially in combining their liberalism with the devotion to theocratic robes which the imperialist militarists who rule Japan have so skilfully thrown about the Throne and the Government. But what one senses in China from the first moment is the feeling of the all-pervading power of Japan which is working as surely as fate to its unhesitating conclusion—the domination of Chinese politics and industry by Japan with a view to its final absorption. It is not my object to analyze the realities of the situation or to inquire whether the universal feeling in China is a collective hallucination or is grounded in fact. The phenomenon is worthy of record on its own account. Even if it be merely psychological, it is a fact which must be reckoned with in both its Chinese and its Japanese aspects. In the first place, as to the differences in psychological atmosphere. Everybody who knows anything about Japan knows that it is the land of reserves and reticences. The half-informed American will tell you that this is put on for the misleading of foreigners. The informed know that it is an attitude shown to foreigners only because it is deeply engrained in the moral and social tradition of Japan; and that, if anything, the Japanese are more likely to be communicative—about many things at least—to a sympathetic foreigner, than to one another. The habit of reserve is so deeply embedded in all the etiquette, convention and daily ceremony of living, as well as in the ideals of strength of character, that only the Japanese who have subjected themselves to foreign influences escape it—and many of them revert. To put it mildly, the Japanese are not a loquacious people; they have the gift of doing rather than of gab.

When accordingly a Japanese statesman or visiting diplomatist engages in unusually prolonged and frank discourse setting forth the aims and procedures of Japan, the student of politics who has been long in the East at once becomes alert, not to say suspicious. A recent illustration is so extreme that it will doubtless seem fantastic beyond belief. But the student at home will have to take these seeming fantasies seriously if he wishes to appreciate the present atmosphere of China. Cables have brought fragmentary reports of some addresses of Baron Goto in America. Doubtless in the American atmosphere these have the effect of reassuring America as to any improper ambitions on the part of Japan. In China, they were taken as announcements that Japan has about completed its plans for the absorption of China, and that the lucubration preliminary to operations of swallowing are about to begin. The reader is forgiven in advance any scepticism he feels about both the fact itself and the correctness of my report of the belief in the alleged fact. His scepticism will not surpass what I should feel in his place. But the suspicion aroused by such statements as this and the recent interview of Foreign Minister Uchida and Baron Ishii must be noted as evidences of the universal belief in China that Japan has one mode of diplomacy for the East and another for the West, and that what is said in the West must be read in reverse in the East.

China, whatever else it is, is not the land of privacies. It is a proverb that nothing long remains secret in China. The Chinese talk more easily than they act—especially in politics. They are adepts in revealing their own shortcomings. They dissect their own weaknesses and failures with the most extraordinary reasonableness. One of the defects upon which they dwell is the love of finding substitutes for positive action, of avoiding entering upon a course of action which might be irrevocable. One almost wonders whether their power of self-criticism is not itself another of these substitutes. At all events, they are frank to the point of loquacity. Between the opposite camps there are always communications flowing. Among official enemies there are "sworn friends." In a land of perpetual compromise, etiquette as well as necessity demands that the ways for later accommodations be kept open. Consequently things which are spoken of only under the breath in Japan are shouted from the housetops in China. It would hardly be good taste in Japan to allude to the report that influential Chinese ministers are in constant receipt of Japanese funds and these corrupt officials are the agencies by which political and economic concessions were wrung from China while Europe and America were busy with the war. But in China nobody even takes the trouble to deny it or even to discuss it. What is psychologically most impressive is the fact that it is merely taken for granted. When it is spoken of, it is as one mentions the heat on an unusually hot day.

In speaking of the feeling of weakness current in Japan about Japan itself, one must refer to the economic situation because of its obvious connection with the international situation. In the first place, there is the strong impression that Japan is over-extended. Even in normal times, Japan relies more upon production for foreign markets than is regarded in most countries as safe policy. And there is the belief that Japan *must* do so, because only by large foreign sellings—large in comparison with the purchasing power of a people still having a low standard of life—can it purchase the raw materials—and even food—it has to have. But during the war, the dependence of manufacturing and trade at home upon the foreign market was greatly increased. The domestic increase of wealth, though very great, is still too much in the hands of the few to affect seriously the internal demand for goods. Item one, which awakens sympathy for Japan as being in a somewhat precarious situation.

Another item concerns the labor situation. Japan seems to feel itself in a dilemma. If she passes even reasonably decent factory laws (or rather attempts their enforcement) and regulates child and women's labor, she will lose that advantage of cheap labor which she now counts on to offset her many disadvantages. On the other hand, strikes, labor difficulties, agitation for unions, etc., are constantly increasing, and the tension in the atmosphere is unmistakable. The rice riots are not often spoken of, but their memory persists, and the fact that they came very near to assuming a directly political aspect. Is there a race between fulfillment of the aspirations of the military clans who still hold the reins, and the growth of genuinely democratic forces which will forever terminate those aspirations? Certainly the defeat of Germany gave a blow to bureaucratic militarism in Japan which in time will go far. Will it have the time required to take effect on foreign policy? The hope that it will is a large factor in stimulating liberal sympathy for a Japan which is beginning to undergo the throes of transition.

As for the direct international situation of Japan, the feeling in Japan is that of the threatening danger of isolation. Germany is gone; Russia is gone. While those facts simplify matters for Japan somewhat, there is also the belief that in taking away potential allies, they have weakened Japan in the general game of balance and counter-balance of power. Particularly does the removal of imperialistic Russia relieve the threat on India which was such a factor in the willingness of Great Britain to make the offensive-defensive alliance. The revelation of the militaristic possibilities of America is another serious factor. Certainly the new triple entente cordiale of Japan, Italy and France is no adequate substitute for a realignment of international forces in which a common understanding between Great Britain and America is a dominant factor. This factor explains, if it does not excuse, some of the querulousness and studied discourtesies with which the Japanese press for some months treated President Wilson, the United States in general and its relation to the League of Nations in particular, while it also throws light on the ardor with which the opportune question of racial discrimination was discussed. (The Chinese have an unfailing refuge in a sense of humor. It was interesting to note the delight with which they received the utterance of the Japanese Foreign Minister, after Japanese success at Paris, that "his attention had recently been called" to various press attacks on America which he much deprecated). In any case there is no mistaking the air of tension and nervous overstrain which now attends all discussion of Japanese foreign relations. In all directions, there are characteristic signs of hesitation, shaking of old beliefs and movement along new lines. Japan seems to be much in the same mood as that which it experienced in the early eighties before, toward the close of that decade, it crystallized its institutions through acceptance of the German constitution, militarism, educational system, and diplomatic methods. So that, once more, the observer gets the impression that substantially all of Japan's energy, abundant as that is, must be devoted to her urgent problems of readjustment.

Come to China, and the difference is incredible. It almost seems as if one were living in a dream; or as if some new Alice had ventured behind an international looking-glass wherein everything is reversed. That we in America should have little idea of the state of things and the frame of mind in China is not astonishing—especially in view of the censorship and the distraction of attention of the last few years. But that Japan and China should be so geographically near, and yet every fact that concerns them appear in precisely opposite perspective, is an experience of a life time. Japanese liberalism? Yes, it is heard of, but only in connection with one form which the longing for the miraculous deus ex machina takes. Perhaps a revolution in Japan may intervene to save China from the fate which now hangs over her. But there is no suggestion that anything less than a complete revolution will alter or even retard the course which is attributed to Japanese diplomacy working hand in hand with Japanese business interests and militarism. The collapse of Russia and Germany? These things only mean that Japan has in a few years fallen complete heir to Russian hopes, achievements and possessions in Manchuria and Outer Mongolia, and has had opportunities in Siberia thrown into her hands which she could hardly have hoped for in her most optimistic moments. And now Japan has, with the blessing of the great Powers at Paris, become also the heir of German concessions, intrigues and ambitions, with added concessions, wrung (or bought) from incompetent and corrupt officials by secret agreements when the world was busy with war. If all the great Powers are so afraid of Japan that they give way to her every wish, what is China that she can escape the doom prepared for her? That is the cry of helplessness going up all over China. And Japanese propagandists take advantage of the situation, pointing to the action of the Peace Conference as proof that the Allies care nothing for China, and that China must throw herself into the arms of Japan if she is to have any protection at all. In short, Japan stands ready as she stood ready in Korea to guarantee the integrity and independence of China. And the fear that the latter must, in spite of her animosity toward Japan, accept this fate in order to escape something worse swims in the sinister air. It is the exact counterpart of the feeling current among the liberals in Japan that Japan has alienated China permanently when a considerate and slower course might have united the two countries. If the economic straits of Japan are alluded to, it is only as a reason why Japan has hurried her diplomatic coercion, her corrupt and secret bargainings with Chinese traitors and her industrial invasion. While the western world supposes that the military and the industrial party in Japan have opposite ideas as to best methods of securing Japanese supremacy in the East, it is the universal opinion in China that they two are working in complete understanding with one another, and the differences that sometimes occur between the Foreign Office in Tokyo and the Ministry of War (which is extra-constitutional in its status) are staged for effect.

These are some of the aspects of the most complete transformation scene that it has ever been the lot of the writer to experience. May it turn out to be only an extraordinary psychological experience! But in the interests of truth it must be recorded that every resident of China, Chinese or American, with whom I have talked in the last four weeks has volunteered the belief that all the seeds of a future great war are now deeply implanted in China. To avert such a calamity they look to the League of Nations or to some other force outside the immediate scene. Unfortunately the press of Japan treats every attempt to discuss the state of opinion in China or the state of facts as evidence that America, having tasted blood in the war, now has its eyes on Asia with the expectation later on of getting its hands on Asia. Consequently America is interested in trying to foster ill-will between China and Japan. If the pro-American Japanese do not enlighten their fellow-countrymen as to the facts, then America ought to return some of the propaganda that visits its shores. But every American who goes to Japan ought also to visit China—if only to complete his education.

[May, 1919.]

II
SHANTUNG, AS SEEN FROM WITHIN

1.

American apologists for that part of the Peace Treaty which relates to China have the advantage of the illusions of distance. Most of the arguments seem strange to anyone who lives in China even for a few months. He finds the Japanese on the spot using the old saying about territory consecrated by treasure spent and blood shed. He reads in Japanese papers and hears from moderately liberal Japanese that Japan must protect China, as well as Japan, against herself, against her own weak or corrupt government, by keeping control of Shantung to prevent China from again alienating that territory to some other power.

The history of European aggression in China gives this argument great force among the Japanese, who for the most part know nothing more about what actually goes on in China than they used to know about Korean conditions. These considerations, together with the immense expectations raised among the Japanese during the war concerning their coming domination of the Far East and the unswerving demand of excited public opinion in Japan during the Versailles Conference for the settlement that actually resulted, give an ironic turn to the statement so often made that Japan may be trusted to carry out her promises. Yes, one is often tempted to say, that is precisely what China fears, that Japan will carry out her promises, for then China is doomed. To one who knows the history of foreign aggression in China, especially the technique of conquest by railway and finance, the irony of promising to keep economic rights while returning sovereignty lies so on the surface that it is hardly irony. China might as well be offered Kant's Critique of Pure Reason on a silver platter as be offered sovereignty under such conditions. The latter is equally metaphysical.

A visit to Shantung and a short residence in its capital city, Tsinan, made the conclusions, which so far as I know every foreigner in China has arrived at, a living thing. It gave a vivid picture of the many and intimate ways in which economic and political rights are inextricably entangled together. It made one realize afresh that only a President who kept himself innocent of any knowledge of secret treaties during the war, could be naïve enough to believe that the promise to return complete sovereignty retaining *only* economic rights is a satisfactory solution. It threw fresh light upon the contention that at most and at worst Japan had only taken over German rights, and that since we had acquiesced in the latter's arrogations we had no call to make a fuss about Japan. It revealed the hollowness of the claim that pro-Chinese propaganda had wilfully misled Americans into confusing the few hundred square miles around the port of Tsing-tao with the Province of Shantung with its thirty millions of Chinese population.

As for the comparison of Germany and Japan one might suppose that the objects for which America nominally entered the war had made, in any case, a difference. But aside from this consideration, the Germans exclusively employed Chinese in the railway shops and for all the minor positions on the railway itself. The railway guards (the difference between police and soldiers is nominal in China) were all Chinese, the Germans merely training them. As soon as Japan invaded Shantung and took over the railway, Chinese workmen and Chinese military guards were at once dismissed and Japanese imported to take their places. Tsinan-fu, the inland terminus of the ex-German railway, is over two hundred miles from Tsing-tao. When the Japanese took over the German railway business office, they at once built barracks, and today there are several hundred soldiers still there—where Germany kept none. Since the armistice even, Japan has erected a powerful military wireless within the grounds of the garrison, against of course the unavailing protest of Chinese authorities. No foreigner can be found who will state that Germany used her ownership of port and railway to discriminate against other nations. No Chinese can be found who will claim that this ownership was used to force the Chinese out of business, or to extend German economic rights beyond those definitely assigned her by treaty. Common sense should also teach even the highest paid propagandist in America that there is, from the standpoint of China, an immense distinction between a national menace located half way around the globe, and one within two days' sail over an inland sea absolutely controlled by a foreign navy, especially as the remote nation has no other foothold and the nearby one already dominates additional territory of enormous strategic and economic value—namely, Manchuria.

These facts bear upon the shadowy distinction between the Tsing-tao and the Shantung claim, as well as upon the solid distinction between German and Japanese occupancy. If there still seemed to be a thin wall between Japanese possession of the port of Tsing-tao and usurpation of Shantung, it was enough to stop off the train in Tsinan-fu to see the wall crumble. For the Japanese wireless and the barracks of the army of occupation are the first things that greet your eyes. Within a few hundred feet of the railway that connects Shanghai, via the important center of Tientsin, with the capital, Peking, you see Japanese soldiers on the nominally Chinese street, guarding their barracks. Then you learn that if you travel upon the ex-German railway towards Tsing-tao, you are ordered to show your passport as if you were entering a foreign country. And as you travel along the road (remembering that you are over two hundred miles from Tsing-tao) you find Japanese soldiers at every station, and several garrisons and barracks at important towns on the line. Then you realize that at the shortest possible notice, Japan could cut all communications between southern China (together with the rich Yangste region) and the capital, and with the aid of the Southern Manchurian Railway at the north of the capital, hold the entire coast and descend at its good pleasure upon Peking.

You are then prepared to learn from eye-witnesses that when Japan made its Twenty-one Demands upon China, machine guns were actually in position at strategic points throughout Shantung, with trenches dug and sandbags placed. You know that the Japanese liberal spoke the truth, who told you, after a visit to China and his return to protest against the action of his government, that the Japanese already had such a military hold upon China that they could control the country within a week, after a minimum of fighting, if war should arise. You also realize the efficiency of official control of information and domestic propaganda as you recall that he also told you that these things were true at the time of his visit, under the Terauchi cabinet, but had been completely reversed by the present Hara ministry. For I have yet to find a single foreigner or Chinese who is conscious of any difference of policy, save as the end of the war has forced the necessity of caution, since other nations can now look China-wards as they could not during the war.

An American can get an idea of the realities of the present situation if he imagines a foreign garrison and military wireless in Wilmington, with a railway from that point to a fortified sea-port controlled by the foreign power, at which the foreign nation can land, without resistance, troops as fast as they can be transported, and with bases of supply, munitions, food, uniforms, etc., already located at Wilmington, at the sea-port and several places along the line. Reverse the directions from south to north, and Wilmington will stand for Tsinan-fu, Shanghai for New York, Nanking for Philadelphia with Peking standing for the seat of government at Washington, and Tientsin for Baltimore. Suppose in addition that the Pennsylvania road is the sole means of communication between Washington and the chief commercial and industrial centers, and you have the framework of the Shantung picture as it presents itself daily to the inhabitants of China. Upon second thought, however, the parallel is not quite accurate. You have to add that the same foreign nation controls also all coast communications from, say, Raleigh southwards, with railway lines both to the nearby coast and to New Orleans. For (still reversing directions) this corresponds to the position of Imperial Japan in Manchuria with its railways to Dairen and through Korea to a port twelve hours sail from a great military center in Japan proper. These are not remote possibilities nor vague prognostications. They are accomplished facts.

Yet the facts give *only* the framework of the picture. What is actually going on within Shantung? One of the demands of the "postponed" group of the Twenty-one Demands was that Japan should supply military and police advisers to China. They are not so much postponed but that Japan enforced specific concessions from China during the war by diplomatic threats to reintroduce their discussion, or so postponed that Japanese advisers are not already installed in the police headquarters of the city of Tsinan, the capital city of Shantung of three hundred thousand population where the Provincial Assembly meets and all the Provincial officials reside. Within recent months the

Japanese consul has taken a company of armed soldiers with him when he visited the Provincial Governor to make certain demands upon him, the visit being punctuated by an ostentatious surrounding of the Governor's yamen by these troops. Within the past few weeks, two hundred cavalry came to Tsinan and remained there while Japanese officials demanded of the Governor drastic measures to suppress the boycott, while it was threatened to send Japanese troops to police the foreign settlement if the demand was not heeded.

A former consul was indiscreet enough to put into writing that if the Chinese Governor did not stop the boycott and the students' movement by force if need be, he would take matters into his own hands. The chief tangible charge he brought against the Chinese as a basis of his demand for "protection" was that Chinese store-keepers actually refused to accept Japanese money in payment for goods, not ordinary Japanese money at that, but the military notes with which, so as to save drain upon the bullion reserves, the army of occupation is paid. And all this, be it remembered, is more than two hundred miles from Tsing-tao and from eight to twelve months after the armistice. Today's paper reports a visit of Japanese to the Governor to inform him that unless he should prevent a private theatrical performance from being given in Tsinan by the students, they would send their own forces into the settlement to protect themselves. And the utmost they might need protection from, was that the students were to give some plays designed to foster the boycott!

Japanese troops overran the Province before they made any serious attempt to capture Tsing-tao. It is only a slight exaggeration to say that they "took" the Chinese Tsinan before they took the German Tsing-tao. Propaganda in America has justified this act on the ground that a German railway to the rear of Japanese forces would have been a menace. As there were no troops but only legal and diplomatic papers with which to attack the Japanese, it is a fair inference that the "menace" was located in Versailles rather than in Shantung, and concerned the danger of Chinese control of their own territory. Chinese have been arrested by Japanese gendarmes in Tsinan and subjected to a torturing third degree of the kind that Korea has made sickeningly familiar. The Japanese claim that the injuries were received while the men were resisting arrest. Considering that there was no more legal ground for arrest than there would be if Japanese police arrested Americans in New York, almost anybody but the pacifist Chinese certainly would have resisted. But official hospital reports testify to bayonet wounds and the marks of flogging. In the interior where the Japanese had been disconcerted by the student propaganda they raided a High School, seized a school boy at random, and took him to a distant point and kept him locked up several days. When the Japanese consul at Tsinan was visited by Chinese officials in protest against these illegal arrests, the consul disclaimed all jurisdiction. The matter, he said, was wholly in the hands of the military authorities in Tsing-tao. His disclaimer was emphasized by the fact that some of the kidnapped Chinese were taken to Tsing-tao for "trial."

The matter of economic rights in relation to political domination will be discussed later in this article. It is no pleasure for one with many warm friends in Japan, who has a great admiration for the Japanese people as distinct from the ruling military and bureaucratic class, to report such facts as have been stated. One might almost say, one might positively say from the standpoint of Japan itself, that the worst thing that can be charged against the policy of Japan in China for the last six years is its immeasurable stupidity. No nation has ever misjudged the national psychology of another people as Japan has that of China. The alienation of China is widespread, deep, bitter. Even the most pessimistic of the Chinese who think that China is to undergo a complete economic and political domination by Japan do not think it can last, even without outside intervention, more than half a century.

Today, at the beginning of a new year, (1920) the boycott is much more complete and efficient than in the most tense days of last summer. Unfortunately, the Japanese policy seems to be under a truly Greek fate which drives it on. Concessions that would have produced a revulsion of feeling in favor of Japan a year ago will now merely salve the surface of the wound. What would have been welcomed even eight months ago would now be received with contempt. There is but one way in which Japan can now restore herself. It is nothing less than complete withdrawal from Shantung, with possibly a strictly commercial concession at Tsing-tao and a real, not a Manchurian, Open Door.

According to the Japanese-owned newspapers published in Tsinan, the Japanese military commander in Tsing-tao recently made a speech to visiting journalists from Tokyo in which he said: "The suspicions of China cannot now be allayed merely by repeating that we have no territorial ambitions in China. We must attain complete economic domination of the Far East. But if Chino-Japanese relations do not improve, some third party will reap the benefit. Japanese residing in China incur the hatred of the Chinese. For they regard themselves as the proud citizens of a conquering country. When the Japanese go into partnership with the Chinese they manage in the greater number of cases to have the profits accrue to themselves. If friendship between China and Japan is to depend wholly upon the government it will come to nothing. Diplomatists, soldiers, merchants, journalists should repent the past. The change must be complete." But it will not be complete until the Japanese withdraw from Shantung leaving their nationals there upon the footing of other foreigners in China.

2.

In discussing the return to China by Japan of a metaphysical sovereignty while economic rights are retained, I shall not repeat the details of German treaty rights as to the railway and the mines. The reader is assumed to be familiar with those facts. The German seizure was outrageous. It was a flagrant case of Might making Right. As von Buelow cynically but frankly told the Reichstag, while Germany did not intend to partition China, she also did not intend to be the passenger left behind in the station when the train started. Germany had the excuse of prior European aggressions, and in turn her usurpation was the precedent for further foreign rape. If judgments are made on a comparative basis, Japan is entitled to all of the white-washing that can be derived from the provocations of European imperialistic powers, including those countries that in domestic policy are democratic. And every fairminded person will recognize that, leaving China out of the reckoning, Japan's proximity to China gives her aggressions the color of self-defence in a way that cannot be urged in behalf of any European power.

It is possible to look at European aggressions in, say, Africa as incidents of a colonization movement. But no foreign policy in Asia can shelter itself behind any colonization plea. For continental Asia is, for practical purposes, India and China, representing two of the oldest civilizations of the globe and presenting two of its densest populations. If there is any such thing in truth as a philosophy of history with its own inner and inevitable logic, one may well shudder to think of what the closing acts of the drama of the intercourse of the West and East are to be. In any case, and with whatever comfort may be derived from the fact that the American continents have not taken part in the aggression and hence may act as a mediator to avert the final tragedy, residence in China forces upon one the realization that Asia is, after all, a large figure in the future reckoning of history. Asia is really here after all. It is not simply a symbol in western algebraic balances of trade. And in the future, so to speak, it is going to be even more here, with its awakened national consciousness of about half the population of the whole globe.

Let the agreements of France and Great Britain made with Japan during the war stand for the measure of western consciousness of the reality of only a small part of Asia, a consciousness generated by the patriotism of Japan backed by its powerful army and navy. The same agreement measures western unconsciousness of the reality of that part of Asia which lies within the confines of China. An even better measure of western unconsciousness may be found perhaps in such a trifling incident as this:—An English friend long resident in Shantung told me of writing indignantly home concerning the British part in the Shantung settlement. The reply came, complacently stating that Japanese ships did so much in the war that the Allies could not properly refuse to recognize Japan's claims. The secret agreements themselves hardly speak as eloquently for the absence of China from the average western consciousness. In saying that China and Asia are to be enormously significant figures in future reckonings, the spectre of a military Yellow Peril is not meant nor even the more credible spectre of an industrial Yellow Peril. But Asia has come to consciousness, and her consciousness of herself will soon be such a massive and persistent thing that it will force itself upon the reluctant consciousness of the west, and lie heavily upon its conscience. And for this fact, China and the western world are indebted to Japan.

These remarks are more relevant to a consideration of the relationship of economic and political rights in Shantung than they perhaps seem. For a moment's reflection will call to mind that all political foreign aggression in China has been carried out for commercial and financial ends, and usually upon some economic pretext. As to the immediate part played by Japan in bringing about a consciousness which will from the present time completely change the relations of the western powers to China, let one little story testify. Some representatives of an English missionary board were making a tour of inspection through China. They went into an interior town in Shantung. They were received with extraordinary cordiality by the entire population. Some time afterwards some of their accompanying friends returned to the village and were received with equally surprising coldness. It came out upon inquiry that the inhabitants had first been moved by the rumor that these people were sent by the British government to secure the removal of the Japanese. Later they were moved by indignation that they had been disappointed.

It takes no forcing to see a symbol in this incident. Part of it stands for the almost incredible ignorance which has rendered China so impotent nationally speaking. The other part of it stands for the new spirit which has been aroused even among the common people in remote districts. Those who fear, or who pretend to fear, a new Boxer movement, or a definite general anti-foreign movement, are, I think, mistaken. The new consciousness goes much deeper. Foreign policies that fail to take it into account and that think that relations with China can be conducted upon the old basis will find this new consciousness obtruding in the most unexpected and perplexing ways.

One might fairly say, still speaking comparatively, that it is part of the bad luck of Japan that her proximity to China, and the opportunity the war gave her to outdo the aggressions of European powers, have made her the first victim of this disconcerting change. Whatever the motives of the American Senators in completely disassociating the United States from the peace settlement as regards China, their action is a permanent asset to China, not only in respect to Japan but with respect to all Chinese foreign relations. Just before our visit to Tsinan, the Shantung Provincial Assembly had passed a resolution of thanks to the American Senate. More significant is the fact that they passed another resolution to be cabled to the English Parliament, calling attention to the action of the American Senate and inviting similar action. China in general and Shantung in particular feels the reinforcement of an external approval. With this duplication, its national consciousness has as it were solidified. Japan is simply the first object to be affected.

The concrete working out of economic rights in Shantung will be illustrated by a single case which will have to stand as typical. Po-shan is an interior mining village. The mines were not part of the German booty; they were Chinese owned. The Germans, whatever their ulterior aims, had made no attempt at dispossessing the Chinese. The mines, however, are at the end of a branch line of the new Japanese owned railway—owned by the government, not by a private corporation, and guarded by Japanese soldiers. Of the forty mines, the Japanese have worked their way, in only four years, into all but four. Different methods are used. The simplest is, of course, discrimination in the use of the railway for shipping. Downright refusal to furnish cars while competitors who accepted Japanese partners got them, is one method. Another more elaborate method is to send but one car when a large number is asked for, and then when it is too late to use cars, send the whole number asked for or even more, and then charge a large sum for demurrage in spite of the fact the mine no longer wants them or has cancelled the order. Redress there is none.

Tsinan has no special foreign concessions. It is, however, a "treaty port" where nationals of all friendly powers can do business. But Po-shan is not even a treaty port. Legally speaking no foreigners can lease land or carry on any business there. Yet the Japanese have forced a settlement as large in area as the entire foreign settlement in the much larger town of Tsinan. A Chinese refused to lease land where the Japanese wished to relocate their railway station. Nothing happened to him directly. But merchants could not get shipping space, or receive goods by rail. Some of them were beaten up by thugs. After a time, they used their influence with their compatriot to lease his land. Immediately the persecutions ceased. Not all the land has been secured by threats or coercion; some has been leased directly by Chinese moved by high prices, in spite of the absence of any legal sanction. In addition, the Japanese have obtained control of the electric light works and some pottery factories, etc.

Now even admitting that this is typical of the methods by which the Japanese plant themselves, a natural American reaction would be to say that, after all, the country is built up industrially by these enterprises, and that though the rights of some individuals may have been violated, there is nothing to make a national, much less an international fuss about. More or less unconsciously we translate foreign incidents into terms of our own experience and environment, and thus miss the entire point. Since America was largely developed by foreign capital to our own economic benefit and without political encroachments, we lazily suppose some such separation of the economic and political to be possible in China. But it must be remembered that China is not an open country. Foreigners can lease land, carry on business, and manufacture only in accord with express treaty agreements. There are no such agreements in the cases typified by the Po-shan incident. We may profoundly disagree with the closed economic policy of China, or we may believe that under existing circumstances it represents the part of prudence for her. That makes no difference. *Given the frequent occurrence of such economic invasions, with the backing of soldiers of the Imperial Army, with the overt aid of the Imperial Railway, and with the refusal of Imperial officials to intervene, there is clear evidence of the attitude and intention of the Japanese government in Shantung.*

Because the population of Shantung is directly confronted with an immense amount of just such evidence, it cannot take seriously the professions of vague diplomatic utterances. What foreign nation is going to intervene to enforce Chinese rights in such a case as Po-shan? Which one is going effectively to call the attention of Japan to such evidences of its failure to carry out its promise? Yet the accumulation of precisely such seemingly petty incidents, and not any single dramatic great wrong, will secure Japan's economic and political domination of Shantung. It is for this reason that foreigners resident in Shantung, no matter in what part, say that they see no sign whatever that Japan is going to get out; that, on the contrary, everything points to a determination to consolidate her position. How long ago was the Portsmouth treaty signed, and what were its nominal pledges about evacuation of Manchurian territory?

Not a month will pass without something happening which will give a pretext for delay, and for making the surrender of Shantung conditional upon this, that and the other thing. Meantime the penetration of Shantung by means of railway discrimination, railway military guards, continual nibblings here and there, will be going on. It would make the chapter too long to speak of the part played by manipulation of finance in achieving this process of attrition of sovereignty. Two incidents must suffice. During the war, Japanese traders with the connivance of their government gathered up immense amounts of copper cash from Shantung and shipped it to Japan against the protests of the Chinese government. What does sovereignty amount to when a country cannot control even its own currency system? In Manchuria the Japanese have forced the introduction of several hundred million dollars of paper currency, nominally, of course, based on a gold reserve. These notes are redeemable, however, only in Japan proper. And there is a law in Japan forbidding the exportation of gold. And there you are.

Japan itself has recently afforded an object lesson in the actual connection of economic and political rights in China. It is so beautifully complete a demonstration that it was surely unconscious. Within the last two weeks, Mr. Obata, the Japanese minister in Peking, has waited upon the government with a memorandum saying that the Foochow incident was the culminating result of the boycott; that if the boycott continues, a series of such incidents is to be apprehended, saying that the situation has become "intolerable" for Japan, and disavowing all responsibility for further consequences unless the government makes a serious effort to stop the boycott. Japan then immediately makes certain specific demands. China must stop the circulation of handbills, the holding of meetings to urge the boycott, the destruction of Japanese goods that have become Chinese property—none have been destroyed that are Japanese owned. Volumes could not say more as to the real conception of Japan of the connection between the economic and the political relations of the two countries. Surely the pale ghost of "Sovereignty" smiled ironically as he read this official note.

President Wilson after having made in the case of Shantung a sharp and complete separation of economic and political rights, also said that a nation boycotted is within sight of surrender. Disassociation of words from acts has gone so far in his case that he will hardly be able to see the meaning of Mr. Obata's communication. The American sense of humor and fair-play may however be counted upon to get its point.

[January, 1920.]

III

HINTERLANDS IN CHINA

One of the two Presidents of China—it is unnecessary to specify which—recently stated that a renewal of the Anglo-Japanese alliance meant a partition of China. In this division, Japan would take the north and Great Britain the south. Probably the remark was not meant to be taken literally in the sense of formal conquest or annexation, but rather symbolically with reference to the tendency of policies and events. Even so, the statement will appear exaggerated or wild to persons outside of China, who either believe that the Open Door policy is now irrevocably established or that Japan is the only foreign Power which China has to fear. But a recent visit to the south revealed that in that section, especially in Canton, the British occupy much the same position of suspicion and dread which is held by the Japanese in the north.

Upon the negative side, the Japanese menace is negligible in the province of Kwantung, in which Canton is situated. There are said to be more Americans in Canton than Japanese, and the American colony is not extensive. Upon the positive side the history of the Cassell collieries contract is instructive. It illustrates the cause of the popular attitude toward the British, and quite possibly explains the bitterness in the remark quoted. The contract is noteworthy from whatever standpoint it is viewed, whether that of time, of the conditions it contains or of the circumstances which accompany it.

Premising that the contract delivers to a British company a monopoly of the rich coal deposits of the province for a period of ninety years and—quite incidentally of course—the right to use all means of transportation, water or rail, wharves and ports now in existence, and also to "construct, manage, superintend and work other roads, railways waterways as may be deemed advisable"—which reads like a monopoly of all further transportation facilities of the province—first take up the time of the making of the contract. It was drawn in April, 1920 and confirmed a few months later. It was made, of course, with the authorities of the Kwantung province, subject to confirmation at Peking. During this period, Kwantung province was governed by military carpet-baggers from the neighboring province of Kwangsei, which was practically alone of the southern provinces allied with the northern government, then under the control of the Anfu party. It was matter of common knowledge that the people of Canton and of the province were bitterly hostile to this outside control and submitted to it only because of military coercion. Civil strife for the expulsion of the outsiders was already going on, continually gaining headway, and a few months later the Kwangsei troops were defeated and expelled from the province by the forces of General Chen, now the civil governor of Kwantung, who received a triumphal ovation upon his entrance into Canton. At this time the present native government was established, a change which made possible the return of Sun Yat Sen and his followers from their exile in Shanghai. It is evident, then, that the collieries contract giving away the natural resources of the people of the province, was knowingly made by a British company with a government which no more represented the people of the province than the military government of Germany represented the people of Belgium during the war.

As to the terms of the contract, the statement that it gave the British company a monopoly of all the coal mines in the province, was not literally accurate. Verbally, twenty-two districts are enumerated. But these are the districts along the lines of the only railways in the province and the only ones soon to be built, including the as yet uncompleted Hankow-Canton railway. Possibly this fact accounts for the anxiety of the British partners in the Consortium that the completion of this line be the first undertaking financed by the Consortium. The document also includes what is perhaps a novelty in legal documents having such a momentous economic importance, namely, the words "etc." after the districts enumerated by name.

For this concession, the British syndicate agreed to pay the provincial government the sum of $1,000,000 (silver of course). This million dollars is to bear six per cent interest to the company, and capital and interest are to be paid back to the company by the provincial government out of the dividends (if any) it is to receive. The nature of these "dividends" is set forth in an article which should receive the careful attention of promoters elsewhere as a model of the possibilities of exploiting contracts.

The ten million capital is divided equally into "A" shares and "B" shares. The "A" shares go unreservedly to the directors of the company, and three millions of the "B" shares are to be allotted by the directors of the company at their discretion. The other two million are again divided into equal portions, one portion representing the sum advanced by the company to the province and to be paid back as just specified, while the other million—one-tenth of the capitalization—is to be a trust fund the dividends of which are to go for the "benefit of the poor people of the province" and for an educational fund for the province. But before any dividends are paid upon the "B" shares, eight per cent dividends are to be paid upon the "A" shares and a *dollar a ton royalty* upon all coal mined. Those having any familiarity with the coal business with its usual royalty of about ten cents a ton can easily calculate the splendid prospects of the "poor people" and the schools, prospects which represent the total return to the provinces of a concession of untold worth. The contract also guarantees to the company the assistance of the provincial government in expropriating the owners of all coal mines which have been granted to other companies but not yet worked. These technical details make dry reading, but they throw light upon the spirit with which the British company undertook its predatory negotiations with a government renounced by the people it professed to govern. In comparison with the relatively crude methods of Japan in Shantung, they show the advantages of wide business experience.

As for the circumstances and context which give added menace to the contract, the following facts are significant. Hong Kong, a British crown colony, lies directly opposite the river upon which Canton is situated. It is the port of export and import for the vast districts served by the mines and railways of the province. It is unnecessary to point out the hold upon all economic development which is given through a monopolistic control of coal. It is hardly too much to say that the enforcement of the contract would enable British interests in Hong Kong to control the entire industrial development of the most flourishing of the provinces of China. It would be a comparatively easy and inexpensive matter to provide the main land with a first class modern harbor and port near Canton. But such a port would tend to reduce the assets of Hong Kong to the possession of the most beautiful scenery in the world. There is already fear that a new harbor will be built. Many persons think that the concession of building such railways etc., "as are deemed advisable for the purpose of the business of the company and to improve those now existing" is the object of the contract, even more than the coal monopoly. For the British already own a considerable part of the mainland, including part of the railway connecting the littoral with Canton. By building a cross-cut from the British owned portion of this railway to the Hankow-Canton line, the latter would become virtually the Hankow-Hong Kong line, and Canton would be a way-station. With the advantages thus secured, the project for building a new port could be indefinitely blocked.

During the period in which the contract was being secured, a congress of British Chambers of Commerce was held in Shanghai. Resolutions were passed in favor of abolishing henceforth the whole principle of special nationalistic concessions, and of cooperating with the Chinese for the upbuilding of China. At the close of the meeting the Chairman announced that a new era for China had finally dawned. All of the British newspapers in China lauded the wise action of the Chambers. At the same time, Mr. Lamont was in Peking, and was setting forth that the object of the Consortium was the abolition of further concessions, and the uniting of the financial resources of the banks in the Consortium for the economic development of China itself. By an ironical coincidence, the Hong Kong-Shanghai Bank, which is the financial power behind the contract and the new company, is the leading British partner in the Consortium. It is difficult to see how the British can henceforth accuse the Japanese of bad faith if any of the banking interests of that country should enter upon independent negotiations with any government in China.

By the time the scene of action was transferred to Peking in order to secure the confirmation of the central government, the Anfu regime was no more, and as yet no confirmation has been secured. The new government at Canton has declined to recognize the contract as having any validity. An official of the Hong Kong government has told an official of the Canton government that the Hong Kong government stands behind the enforcement of the contract, and that Kwantung province is a British

Hinterland. Within the last few weeks the Governor of Hong Kong and a leading Chinese banker of Hong Kong who is a British subject have visited Peking. Rumors were rife in the south as to the object of the visit. British sources published the report that one object was to return Weihaiwei to China—in case Peking agreed to turn over more of the Kwantung mainland to Hong Kong as a quid pro quo. Chinese opinion in the south was that one main object was to secure the Peking confirmation of the Cassell contract, in which case $900,000 more would be forthcoming, $100,000 having been paid down when the contract was signed with the provincial government. Peking does not recognize the present Canton government but regards it as an outlaw. The crowd that signed the contract is still in control of the neighboring province of Kwangsei and they are relied upon by the north to effect the military subjugation of the seceded province. Fighting has already, indeed, begun, but the Kwangsei militarists are badly in need of money; if Peking ratifies the contract, a large part of the funds will be paid over to them—all that isn't lost by the wayside to the northern militarists.[1] Meantime British news agencies keep up a constant circulation of reports tending to discredit the Kwantung government, although all impartial observers on the spot regard it as altogether the most promising one in China.

These considerations not only throw light on some of the difficulties of the functioning of the Consortium, but they give an indispensable background for judging the actual effect of the renewal of the Anglo-Japanese alliance. By force of circumstances each government, even against its own wish, will be compelled to wink at the predatory policies of the other; and the tendency will be to create a division of spheres of influence between the north and south in order to avoid more direct conflicts. The English liberals who stand for the renewal of the alliance on the ground that it will enable England to exercise a check on Japanese policies, are more naïve than was Mr. Wilson with his belief in the separation of the economic and

---

1 Since the text was written, the newspapers have stated that the Peking Government has officially refused to validate the agreement.

political control of Shantung.

It cannot be too often repeated that the real point of friction between the United States and Japan is not in California but in China. It is silly—unless it is calculated—for English authorities to keep repeating that under no circumstances does the alliance mean that Great Britain would support Japan in a war with the United States. The day the alliance is renewed, the hands of the militarists in Japan will be strengthened and the hands of the liberals—already weak enough—be still further weakened. In consequence, all the sources of friction in China between the United States and Japan will be intensified. I do not believe in the predicted war. But should it come, the first act of Japan—so everyone in China believes—will be to seize the ports of northern China and its railways in order to make sure of an uninterrupted supply of food and raw materials. The act would be justified as necessary to national existence. Great Britain in alliance with Japan would be in no position to protest in anything but the most perfunctory way. The guarantee of such abstinence would be for Japan the next best thing to open naval and financial support. Without the guarantee they would not dare the seizure of Chinese ports. In recent years diplomatists have shown themselves capable of unlimited stupidity. But it is not possible that the men in the British Foreign Office are not aware of these elementary facts. If they renew the alliance they knowingly take the responsibility for the consequences.

[May 24, 1921.]

IV

A POLITICAL UPHEAVAL IN CHINA

Even in America we have heard of one Chinese revolution, that which thrust the Manchu dynasty from the throne. The visitor in China gets used to casual references to the second revolution, that which frustrated Yuan Shi Kai's aspirations to be emperor, and the third, the defeat in 1917 of the abortive attempt to put the Manchu boy emperor back into power. And within the last few weeks the (September 1920) fourth upheaval has taken place. It may not be dignified by the name of the fourth revolution, for the head of the state has not been changed by it. But as a manifestation of the forces that shape Chinese political events, for evil and for good, perhaps this last disturbance surpasses the last two "revolutions" in significance.

Chinese politics in detail are highly complicated, a mess of personalities and factions whose oscillations no one can follow who does not know a multitude of personal, family and provincial histories. But occasionally something happens which simplifies the tangle. Definite outlines frame themselves out of the swirling criss-cross of strife, intrigue and ambition. So, at present, the complete collapse of the Anfu clique which owned the central government for two years marks the end of that union of internal militarism and Japanese foreign influence which was, for China, the most marked fruit of the war. When China entered the war a "War Participation" army was formed. It never participated; probably it was never meant to. But its formation threw power wholly into the hands of the military clique, as against the civilian constitutionalists. And in return for concessions, secret agreements relating to Manchuria, Shantung, new railways, etc., Japan supplied money, munitions, instructors for the army and a benevolent supervision of foreign and domestic politics. The war came to an unexpected and untimely end, but by this time the offspring of the marriage of the militarism of Yuan Shi Kai and Japanese money and influence was a lusty youth. Bolshevism was induced to take the place of Germany as a menace requiring the keeping up of the army, and loans and teachers. Mongolia was persuaded to cut her strenuous ties with Russia, to renounce her independence and come again under Chinese sovereignty.

The army and its Japanese support and instruction was, accordingly, continued. In place of the "War Participation" army appeared the "Frontier Defense" army. Marshal Tuan, the head of the military party, remained the nominal political power behind the presidential chair, and General Hsu (commonly known as little Hsu, in distinction from old Hsu, the president) was the energetic manager of the Mongolian adventure which, by a happy coincidence, required a bank, land development companies and railway schemes, as well as an army. About this military centre as a nucleus gathered the vultures who fed on the carrion. This flock took the name of the Anfu Club. It did not control the entire cabinet, but to it belonged the Minister of Justice, who manipulated the police and the courts, persecuted the students, suppressed liberal journals and imprisoned inconvenient critics. And the Club owned the ministers of finance and communications, the two cabinet places that dispense revenues, give out jobs and make loans. It also regulated the distribution of intelligence by mail and telegraph. The reign of corruption and despotic inefficiency, tempered only by the student revolt, set in. In two years the Anfu Club got away with two hundred millions of public funds directly, to say nothing of what was wasted by incompetency and upon the army. The Allies had set out to get China into the war. They succeeded in getting Japan into control of Peking and getting China, politically speaking, into a seemingly hopeless state of corruption and confusion.

The militaristic or Pei-Yang party was, however, divided into two factions, each called after a province. The Anwhei party gathered about little Hsu and was almost identical with the Anfus. The Chili faction had been obliged, so far as Peking was concerned, to content itself with such leavings as the Anfu Club tossed to it. Apparently it was hopelessly weaker than its rival, although Tuan, who was personally honest and above financial scandal, was supported by both factions and was the head of both. About three months ago there were a few signs that, while the Anfu Club had been entrenching itself in Peking, the rival faction had been quietly establishing itself in the provinces. A league of Eight Tuchuns (military governors of the provinces) came to the assistance of the president against some unusually strong pressure from the Anfu Club. In spite of the fact that the military governor of the three Manchurian provinces, Chang Tso Lin, popularly known as the Emperor of Manchuria, lined up with this league, practically nobody expected anything except some manœuvering to get a larger share of the spoils.

But late in June the president invited Chang Tso Lin to Peking. The latter saw Tuan, told him that he was surrounded by evil advisers, demanded that he cut loose from little Hsu and the Anfu Club, and declared open war upon little Hsu—the two had long and notoriously been bitter enemies. Even then people had great difficulty in believing that anything would happen except another Chinese compromise. The president was known to be sympathetic upon the whole with the Chili faction, but the president, if not a typical Chinese, is at least typical of a certain kind of Chinese mandarin, non-resistant, compromising, conciliating, procrastinating, covering up, evading issues, face-saving. But finally something happened. A mandate was issued dismissing little Hsu from office, military and civil, dissolving the frontier defense corps as such, and bringing it under the control of the Ministry of War (usually armies in China belong to some general or Tuchun, not to the country). For almost forty-eight hours it was thought that Tuan had consented to sacrifice little Hsu and that the latter would submit at least temporarily. Then with equally sensational abruptness Tuan brought pressure to bear on the president. The latter was appointed head of a national defense army, and rewards were issued for the heads of the chiefs of the Chili faction, nothing, however, being said about Chang Tso Lin, who had meanwhile returned to Mukden and who still professed allegiance to Tuan. Troops were mobilized; there was a rush of officials and of the wealthy to the concessions of Tientsin and to the hotels of the legation quarter.

This sketch is not meant as history, but simply as an indication of the forces at work. Hence it is enough to say that two weeks after Tuan and little Hsu had intimidated the president and proclaimed themselves the saviors of the Republic, they were in hiding, their enemies of the Chili party were in complete control of Peking, and rewards from fifty thousand dollars down were offered for the arrest of little Hsu, the ex-ministers of justice, finance and communications, and other leaders of the Anfu Club. The political turnover was as complete as it was sensational. The seemingly impregnable masters of China were impotent fugitives. The carefully built up Anfu Club, with its military, financial and foreign support, had crumbled and fallen. No country at any time has ever seen a political upheaval more sudden and more thoroughgoing. It was not so much a defeat as a dissolution like that of death, a total disappearance, an evaporation.

Corruption had worked inward, as it has a way of doing. Japanese-bought munitions would not explode; quartermasters vanished with the funds with which stores were to be bought; troops went without anything to eat for two or three days; large numbers, including the larger part of one division, went over to the enemy en masse; those who did not desert had no heart for fighting and ran away or surrendered on the slightest provocation, saying they were willing to fight for their country but saw no reason why they should fight for a faction, especially a faction that had been selling the country to a foreign nation. In the manner of the defeat of the Anfu clique at the height of its supremacy, rather than in the mere fact of its defeat, lies the credit side of the Chinese political balance sheet. It is a striking exhibition of the oldest and best faith of the Chinese—the power of moral considerations. Public opinion, even that of the coolie on the street, was wholly against the Anfu party. It went down not so much because of the strength of the other side as because of its own rottenness.

So far the results are to all appearances negative. The most marked is the disappearance of Japanese prestige. As one of the leading men in the War Office said: "For over a year now the people have been strongly opposed to the Japanese government on account of Shantung. But now even the generals do not care for Japan any more." It is hardly logical to take the easy collapse of the Japanese-supported Anfu party as a proof of the weakness of Japan, but prestige is always a matter of feeling rather than of logic. Many who were intimidated to the point of hypnotism by the idea of the irresistible power of Japan are now freely laughing at the inefficiency of Japanese leadership. It would not be safe to predict that Japan will not come back as a force to be reckoned with in the internal as well as external politics of China, but it is safe to say that never again will Japan figure as superman to China. And such a negation is after all a positive result.

And so in its way is the overthrow of the Anwhei faction of the militarist party. The Chinese liberals do not feel very optimistic about the immediate outcome. They have mostly given up the idea that the country can be reformed by political means. They are sceptical about the possibility of reforming even politics until a new generation comes on the scene. They are now putting their faith in education and in social changes which will take some years to consummate themselves visibly. The self-styled southern republican constitutional party has not shown itself in much better light than the northern militarist party. In fact, its old leader Sun Yat Sen now cuts one of the most ridiculous figures in China, as shortly before this upheaval he had definitely aligned himself with Tuan and little Hsu.[2]

This does not mean, however, that democratic opinion thinks nothing has been gained. The demonstration of the inherent weakness of corrupt militarism will itself prevent the development of any militarism as complete as that of the Anfus. As one Chinese gentleman said to me: "When Yuan Shi Kai was overthrown, the tiger killed the lion. Now a snake has killed the tiger. No matter how vicious the snake may become, some smaller animal will be able to kill him, and his life will be shorter than that of either lion or tiger." In short, each successive upheaval brings nearer the day when civilian supremacy will be established. This result will be achieved partly because

2   This was written of course several months before Sun Yat Sen was reinstated in control of Canton by the successful revolt of his local adherents against the southern militarists who had usurped power and driven out Sun Yat Sen and his followers. But up to the time when I left China, in July of this year, it was true that the liberals of northern and central China who were bitterly opposed to the Peking Government, did not look to the Southern Government with much hope. The common attitude was a "plague upon both of your houses" and a desire for a new start. The conflict between North and South looms much larger in the United States than it did in China.

of the repeated demonstrations of the uncongeniality of military despotism to the Chinese spirit, and partly because with every passing year education will have done its work. Suppressed liberal papers are coming to life, while over twenty Anfu subsidized newspapers and two subsidized news agencies have gone out of being. The soldiers, including many officers in the Anwhei army, clearly show the effects of student propaganda. And it is worth while to note down the name of one of the leaders on the victorious side, the only one whose troops did any particular fighting, and that against great odds in numbers. The name is Wu Pei Fu. He at least has not fought for the Chili faction against the Anwhei faction. He has proclaimed from the first that he was fighting to rid the country of military control of civil government, and against traitors who would sell their country to foreigners. He has come out strongly for a new popular assembly, to form a new constitution and to unite the country. And although Chang Tso Lin has remarked that Wu Pei Fu as a military subordinate could not be expected to intervene in politics, he has not as yet found it convenient to oppose the demand for a popular assembly. Meanwhile the liberals are organizing their forces, hardly expecting to win a victory, but resolved, win or lose, to take advantage of the opportunity to carry further the education of the Chinese people in the meaning of democracy.

[August, 1920.]

V

DIVIDED CHINA

1.

In January 1920 the Peking government issued an edict proclaiming the unification of China. On May 5th Sun Yat Sen was formally inaugurated in Canton as president of all China. Thus China has within six months been twice unified, once from the northern standpoint and once from the southern. Each act of "unification" is in fact a symbol of the division of China, a division expressing differences of language, temperament, history, and political policy as well as of geography, persons and factions. This division has been one of the outstanding facts of Chinese history since the overthrow of the Manchus ten years ago and it has manifested itself in intermittent civil war. Yet there are two other statements which are equally true, although they flatly contradict each other and the one just made. One statement is that so far as the people of China are concerned there is no real division on geographical lines, but only the common division occurring everywhere between conservatives and progressives. The other is that instead of two divisions in China, there are at least five, two parties in both the north and south, and another in the central or Yangtse region,[3] each one of the five splitting up again more or less on factional and provincial lines. And so far as the future is concerned, probably this last statement is the most significant of the three. That all three statements are true is what makes Chinese politics so difficult to understand even in their larger features.

By the good fortune of circumstances we were in Canton when the inauguration occurred. Peking and Canton are a long way apart in more than distance. There is little exchange of actual news between the two places; what filters through into either city and gets published consists mostly of rumors tending

---

3   Since the writing of this and the former chapter there are some signs that Wu Pei Fu wants to set up in control of the middle districts.

to discredit the other city. In Canton, the monarchy is constantly being restored in Peking; and in Peking, Canton is Bolshevized at least once a week, while every other week open war breaks out between the adherents of Sun Yat Sen, and General Chen Kwang Ming, the civil governor of the province. There is nothing to give the impression—even in circles which accept the Peking government only as an evil necessity—that the pretensions of Sun Yat Sen represent anything more than the desires of a small and discredited group to get some slight power for themselves at the expense of national unity. Even in Fukien, the province next north of Kwantung, one found little but gossip whose effect was to minimize the importance of the southern government. In foreign circles in the north as well as in liberal Chinese circles upon the whole, the feeling is general that bad as the de facto Peking government may be, it represents the cause of national unity, while the southern government represents a perpetuation of that division of China which makes her weak and which offers the standing invitation to foreign intrigue and aggression. Only occasionally during the last few months has some returned traveller timidly advanced the opinion that we had the "wrong dope" on the south, and that they were really trying "to do something down there."

Consequently there was little preparation on my part for the spectacle afforded in Canton during the week of May 5th. This was the only demonstration I have seen in China during the last two years which gave any evidence of being a spontaneous popular movement. New Yorkers are accustomed to crowds, processions, street decorations and accompanying enthusiasm. I doubt if New York has ever seen a demonstration which surpassed that of Canton in size, noise, color or spontaneity—in spite of tropical rains. The country people flocked in in such masses, that, being unable to find accommodation even in the river boats, they kept up a parade all night. Guilds and localities which were not able to get a place in the regular procession organized minor ones on their own account on the day before and after the official demonstration. Making all possible allowance for the intensity of Cantonese local loyalty and the fact that they might be celebrating a Cantonese affair rather than a principle, the scene was sufficiently impressive to revise one's preconceived ideas and to make one try to find out what it is that gives the southern movement its vitality.

A demonstration may be popular and still be superficial in significance. However one found foreigners on the ground—at least Americans—saying that in the last few months the men in power in Canton were the only officials in China who were actually doing something for the people instead of filling their own pockets and magnifying their personal power. Even the northern newspapers had not entirely omitted reference to the suppression of licensed gambling. On the spot one learned that this suppression was not only genuine and thorough, but that it meant a renunciation of an annual revenue of nearly ten million dollars on the part of a government whose chief difficulty is financial, and where—apart from motives of personal squeeze—it would have been easy to argue that at least temporarily the end justified the means in retaining this source of revenue. English papers throughout China have given much praise to the government of Hong Kong because it has cut down its opium revenue from eight to four millions annually with the plan for ultimate extinction. Yet Hong Kong is prosperous, it has not been touched by civil war, and it only needs revenue for ordinary civil purposes, not as a means of maintaining its existence in a crisis.

Under the circumstances, the action of the southern government was hardly less than heroic. This renunciation is the most sensational act of the Canton government, but one soon learns that it is the accompaniment of a considerable number of constructive administrative undertakings. Among the most notable are attempts to reform the local magistracies throughout the province, the establishment of municipal government in Canton—something new in China where local officials are all centrally appointed and controlled—based upon the American Commission plan, and directed by graduates of schools of political science in the United States; plans for introducing local self-government throughout the province; a scheme for introduction of universal primary education in Canton to be completed in three steps.

These reforms are provincial and local. They are part of a general movement against centralization and toward local autonomy which is gaining headway all over China, a protest against the appointment of officials from Peking and the management of local affairs in the interests of factions—and pocket-books—whose chief interest in local affairs is what can be extracted in the way of profit. For the only analogue of provincial government in China at the present time is the carpet bag government of the south in the days following our civil war. These things explain the restiveness of the country, including central as well as southern provinces, under Peking domination. But they do not explain the setting up of a new national, or federal government, with the election of Mr. Sun Yat Sen as its president. To understand this event it is necessary to go back into history.

In June, 1917, the parliament in Peking was about to adopt a constitution. The parliament was controlled by leaders of the old revolutionary party who had been at loggerheads with Yuan and with the executive generally. The latter accused them of being obstructionists, wasting time in discussing and theorizing when the country needed action. Japan had changed her tactics regarding the participation of China in the war, and having got her position established through the Twenty-one Demands, saw a way of controlling Chinese arsenals and virtually amalgamating the Chinese armies with her own through supervising China's entrance into the war. The British and French were pressing desperately for the same end. Parliament was slow to act, and Tang Shao Yi, Sun Yat Sen and other southern leaders were averse, since they regarded the war as none of China's business and were upon the whole more anti-British than anti-German—a fact which partly accounts for the share of British journals in the present press propaganda against the Canton government. But what brought matters to a head was the fact that the constitution which was about to be adopted eliminated the military governors or tuchuns of the provinces, and restored the supremacy of civil authority which had been destroyed by Yuan Shi Kai, in addition to introducing a policy of decentralization. Coached by members of the so-called progressive party which claimed to be constitutionalist and which had a factionalist interest in overthrowing the revolutionaries who controlled the legislative branch if not the executive, the military governors demanded that the president suspend parliament and dismiss the legislators. This demand was more than passively supported by all the Allied diplomats

in Peking with the honorable exception of the American legation. The president weakly yielded and issued an edict dispel-
ling parliament, virtually admitting in the document the
illegality of his action. Less than a month afterwards he was a
refugee in the Dutch legation on account of the farce of monarchical restoration staged by Chang Shun—who at the present
time is again coming to the front in the north as adjutant to the
plans of Chang Tso Lin, the present "strong man" of China.
Later, elections were held and a new parliament elected. This
parliament has been functioning as the legislature of China at
Peking and elected the president, Hsu Shi Chang, the head of
the government recognized by the foreign Powers—in short it is
the Chinese government from an international standpoint, the
Peking government from a domestic standpoint.

The revolutionary members of the old parliament never
recognized the legality of their dispersal, and consequently refused to admit the legal status of the new parliament, called by
them the bogus parliament, and of the president elected by it,
especially as the new legislative body was not elected according
to the rules laid down by the constitution. Under the lead of
some of the old members, the old parliament, called by its oppo-
nents the defunct parliament, has led an intermittent existence
ever since. Claiming to be the sole authentic constitutional
body of China, it finally elected Dr. Sun president of China and
thus prepared the act of the fifth of May, already reported.

Such is the technical and formal background of the present
southern government. Its attack upon the legality of the Peking
government is doubtless technically justified. But for various
reasons its own positive status is open to equally grave doubts.
The terms "bogus" and "defunct," so freely cast at each other,
both seem to an outsider to be justified. It is less necessary to go
into the reasons which appear to invalidate the position of the
southern parliament because of the belated character of its final action. A protest which waits four years to assert itself in
positive action is confronted not with legal technicalities but
with accomplished facts. In my opinion, legality for legality, the
southern government has a bare shade the better of the technical argument. But in the face of a government which has
foreign recognition and which has maintained itself after a
fashion for four years, a legal shadow is a precarious political

basis. It is wiser to regard the southern government as a revolutionary government, which in addition to the prestige of continuing the revolutionary movement of ten years ago has also a considerable sentimental asset as a protest of constitutionalism against the military usurpations of the Peking government.

It is an open secret that the southern movement has not received the undivided support of all the forces present in Canton which are opposed to the northern government. Tang Shao Yi, for example, was notable for his absence at the time of the inauguration, having found it convenient to visit the graves of his ancestors at that time. The provincial governor, General Chen Kwang Ming, was in favor of confining efforts to the establishment of provincial autonomy and the encouragement of similar movements in other provinces, looking forward to an eventual federal, or confederated, government of at least all the provinces south of the Yangtse. Many of his generals wanted to postpone action until Kwantung province had made a military alliance with the generals in the other southwestern provinces, so as to be able to resist the north should the latter undertake a military expedition. Others thought the technical legal argument for the new move was being overworked, and while having no objections to an out and out revolutionary movement against Peking, thought that the time for it had not yet come. They are counting on Chang Tso Lin's attempting a monarchical restoration and think that the popular revulsion against that move would create the opportune time for such a movement as has now been prematurely undertaken. However in spite of reports of open strife freely circulated by British and Peking government newspapers, most of the opposition elements are now loyally suppressing their opposition and supporting the government of Sun Yat Sen. A compromise has been arranged by which the federal government will confine its attention to foreign affairs, leaving provincial matters wholly in the hands of Governor Chen and his adherents. There is still room for friction however, especially as to the control of revenues, since at present there are hardly enough funds for one administration, let alone two.

2.

The members of the new southern government are strikingly different in type from those one meets elsewhere whether in Peking or the provincial capitals. The latter men are literally mediaeval when they are not late Roman Empire, though most of them have learned a little modern patter to hand out to foreigners. The former are educated men, not only in the school sense and in the sense that they have had some special training for their jobs, but in the sense that they think the ideas and speak the language current among progressive folk all over the world. They welcome inquiry and talk freely of their plans, hopes and fears. I had the opportunity of meeting all the men who are most influential in both the local and federal governments; these conversations did not take the form of interviews for publication, but I learned that there are at least three angles from which the total situation is viewed.

Governor Chen has had no foreign education and speaks no English. He is distinctively Chinese in his training and outlook. He is a man of force, capable of drastic methods, straightforward intellectually and physically, of unquestioned integrity and of almost Spartan life in a country where official position is largely prized for the luxuries it makes possible. For example, practically alone among Chinese provincial officials of the first rank he has no concubines. Not only this, but he proposed to the provincial assembly a measure to disenfranchise all persons who have concubines. (The measure failed because it is said its passage would have deprived the majority of the assemblymen of their votes.) He is by all odds the most impressive of all the officials whom I have met in China. If I were to select a man likely to become a national figure of the first order in the future, it would be, unhesitatingly, Governor Chen. He can give and also command loyalty—a fact which in itself makes him almost unique.

His views in gist are as follows: The problem of problems in China is that of real unification. Industry and education are held back because of lack of stability of government, and the better elements in society seclude themselves from all public effort. The question is how this unification is to be obtained. In the past it has been tried by force used by strong individuals.

Yuan Shi Kai tried and failed; Feng Kuo Chang tried and failed; Tuan Chi Jui tried and failed. That method must be surrendered. China can be unified only by the people themselves, employing not force but the methods of normal political evolution. The only way to engage the people in the task is to decentralize the government. Futile efforts at centralization must be abandoned. Peking and Canton alike must allow the provinces the maximum of autonomy; the provincial capitals must give as much authority as possible to the districts, and the districts to the communities. Officials must be chosen by and from the local districts and everything must be done to encourage local initiative. Governor Chen's chief ambition is to introduce this system into Kwantung province. He believes that other provinces will follow as soon as the method has been demonstrated, and that national unity will then be a pyramid built out of the local blocks.

With extreme self-government in administrative matters, Governor Chen will endeavor to enforce a policy of centralized economic control. He says in effect that the west has developed economic anarchy along with political control, with the result of capitalistic domination and class struggle. He wishes to avert this consequence in China by having government control from the first of all basic raw materials and all basic industries, mines, transportation, factories for cement, steel, etc. In this way the provincial authorities hope to secure an equable industrial development of the province, while at the same time procuring ample revenues without resorting to heavy taxation. Since almost all the other governors in China are using their power, in combination with the exploiting capitalists native and foreign, to monopolize the natural resources of their provinces for private profit, it is not surprising that Governor Chen's views are felt to be a menace to privilege and that he is advertised all over China as a devout Bolshevist. His views have special point in view of British efforts to get an economic stranglehold upon the province—efforts which are dealt with in a prior chapter.

Another type of views lays chief stress upon the internal political condition of China. Its adherents say in effect: Why make such a fuss about having two governments for China, when, in point of fact, China is torn into dozens of governments? In the north, war is sure to break out sooner or later between Chang Tso Lin and his rivals. Each military governor is afraid of his division generals. The brigade generals intrigue against the division leaders, and even colonels are doing all they can to further their personal power. The Peking government is a stuffed sham, taking orders from the military governors of the provinces, living only on account of jealousies among these generals, and by the grace of foreign diplomatic support. It is actually bankrupt, and this actual state will soon be formally recognized. The thing for us to do is to go ahead, maintain in good faith the work of the revolution, give this province the best possible civil administration; then in the inevitable approaching débâcle, the southern government will be ready to serve as the nucleus of a genuine reconstruction. Meantime we want, if not the formal recognition of foreign governments, at least their benevolent neutrality.

Dr. Sun still embodies in himself the spirit of the revolution of 1911. So far as that was not anti-Manchu it was in essence nationalistic, and only accidentally republican. The day after the inauguration of Dr. Sun, a memorial was dedicated to the seventy-two patriot heroes who fell in an abortive attempt in Canton to throw off the Manchu yoke, some six months before the successful revolt. The monument is the most instructive single lesson which I have seen in the political history of the revolution. It is composed of seventy-two granite blocks. Upon each is engraved: Given by the Chinese National League of Jersey City, or Melbourne, or Mexico, or Liverpool, or Singapore, etc. Chinese nationalism is a product of Chinese migration to foreign countries; Chinese nationalism on foreign shores financed the revolution, and largely furnished its leaders and provided its organization. Sun Yat Sen was the incarnation of this nationalism, which was more concerned with freeing China—and Asia—from all foreign domination than with particular political problems. And in spite of the movement of events since that day, he remains essentially at that stage, being closer in spirit to the nationalists of the European irredentist type than to the spirit of contemporary young China. A convinced republican, he nevertheless measures events and men in the concrete by what he thinks they will do to promote the independence of China from foreign control, rather than by what they will do to promote a truly democratic government. This is the sole explanation that can be given for his unfortunate coquetting a year ago with the leaders of the now fallen Anfu Club. He allowed himself to be deceived into thinking that they were ready to turn against the Japanese if he would give them his support; and his nationalist imagination was inflamed by the grandiose schemes of little Hsu for the Chinese subjugation of Mongolia.

More openly than others, Dr. Sun admits and justifies the new southern government as representing a division of China. If, he insists, it had not been for the secession of the south in 1917, Japan would now be in virtually complete control of all China. A unified China would have meant a China ready to be swallowed whole by Japan. The secession localized Japanese aggressions, made it evident that the south would fight rather than be devoured, and gave a breathing spell in which public opinion in the north rallied against the Twenty-one Demands and against the military pact with Japan. Thus it saved the independence of China. But, while it checked Japan, it did not checkmate her. She still expects with the assistance of Chang Tso Lin to make northern China her vassal. The support which foreign governments in general and the United States in particular are giving Peking is merely playing into the hands of the Japanese. The independent south affords the only obstacle which causes Japan to pause in her plan of making northern China in effect a Japanese province. A more than usually authentic rumor says that upon the occasion of the visit of the Japanese consul general to the new president (no other foreign official has made an official visit), the former offered from his government the official recognition of Dr. Sun as president of all China, if the latter would recognize the Twenty-one Demands as an accomplished fact. From the Japanese standpoint the offer was a safe one, as this acceptance of Japanese claims is the one thing impossible to the new government. But meantime the offer naturally confirms the nationalists of Dr. Sun's type in their belief that the southern split is the key to maintaining the political independence of China; or, as Dr. Sun puts it, that a divided China is for the time being the only means to an ultimately independent China.

These views are not given as stating the whole truth of the

situation. They are ex parte. But they are given as setting forth in good faith the conceptions of the leaders of the southern movement and as requiring serious attention if the situation of China, domestic and international, is to be understood. Upon my own account, and not simply as expressing the views of others, I have reached a conclusion quite foreign to my thought before I visited the south. While it is not possible to attach too much importance to the unity of China as a part of the foreign policy of the United States, it is possible to attach altogether too much importance to the Peking government as a symbol of that unity. To borrow and adapt the words of one southern leader, while the United States can hardly be expected to do other than recognize the Peking as the de facto government, there is no need to coddle that government and give it face. Such a course maintains a nominal and formal unity while in fact encouraging the military and corrupt forces that keep China divided and which make for foreign aggression.

In my opinion as the outcome of two years' observation of the Chinese situation, the real interests of both China and the United States would be served if, in the first place, the United States should take the lead in securing from the diplomatic body in Peking the serving of express notice upon the Peking government that in no case would a restoration of the monarchy be recognized by the Powers. This may seem in America like an unwarranted intervention in the domestic affairs of a foreign country. But in fact such intervention is already a fact. The present government endures only in virtue of the support of foreign Powers. The notice would put an end to one kind of intrigue, one kind of rumor and suspicion, which is holding industry and education back and which is keeping China in a state of unrest and instability. It would establish a period of comparative quiet in which whatever constructive forces exist may come to the front. The second measure would be more extreme. The diplomacy of the United States should take the lead in making it clear that unless the promises about the disbanding of the army, and the introduction of general retrenchment are honestly and immediately carried out, the Powers will pursue a harsh rather than a benevolent policy toward the Peking government, insisting upon immediate payment of interest and loans as they fall due and holding up the government to the strictest meeting of all its obligations. The notification to be effective might well include a virtual threat of withdrawal of recognition in case the government does not seriously try to put its profuse promises into execution. It should also include a definite discouragement of any expenditures designed for military conquest of the south.

Diplomatic recognition of the southern government is out of the question at present. It is not out of the question to put on the financial screws so that the southern government will be allowed space and time to demonstrate what it can do by peaceful means to give one or more provinces a decent, honest and progressive civil administration. It is unnecessary to enumerate the obstacles in the way of carrying out such a policy. But in my judgment it is the only policy by which the Great Powers will not become accomplices in perpetuating the weakness and division of China. It is the most straightforward way of meeting whatever plans of aggression Japan may entertain.

[May, 1921.]

VI
Federalism in China

The newcomer in China in observing and judging events usually makes the mistake of attaching too much significance to current happenings. Occurrences take place which in the western world would portend important changes—and nothing important results. It is not easy to loosen the habit of years; and so the visitor assumes that an event which is striking to the point of sensationalism must surely be part of a train of events having a definite trend; some deep-laid plan must be behind it. It takes a degree of intellectual patience added to time and experience to make one realize that even when there is a rhythm in events the tempo is so retarded that one must wait a long time to judge what is really going on. Most political events are like daily changes in the weather, fluctuations back and forth which may seriously affect individuals but which taken one by one tell little about the movement of the seasons. Even the occurrences which are due to human intention are usually sporadic and casual, and the observer errs by reading into them too much plot, too comprehensive a scheme, too farsighted a plan. The aim behind the event is likely to be only some immediate advantage, some direct increase of power, the overthrow of a rival, the grasping at greater wealth by an isolated act, without any consecutive or systematic looking ahead.

Foreigners are not the only ones who have erred, however, in judging the Chinese political situation of the last few years. Beginning two years ago, one heard experienced Chinese with political affiliations saying that it was impossible for things to go on as they were for more than three months longer. Some decisive change must occur. Yet outwardly the situation has remained much the same not only for three months but for two years, the exception being the overthrow of the Anfu faction a year ago. And this occurrence hardly marked a definite turn in events, as it was, to a considerable extent, only a shifting of power from the hands of one set of tuchuns to another set. Nevertheless at the risk of becoming a victim of the fallacy which I have been setting forth, I will hazard the remark that the last few months *have* revealed a definite and enduring trend—that through the diurnal fluctuations of the strife for personal power and wealth a seasonal political change in society is now showing itself. Certain lines of cleavage seem to show themselves, so that through the welter of striking, picturesque, sensational but meaningless events, a definite pattern is revealed.

This pattern is indicated by the title of this chapter—a movement toward the development of a federal form of government. In calling the movement one toward federalism, there is, however, more of a jump into the remote future than circumstances justify. It would be more accurate, as well as more modest, to say that there is a well defined and seemingly permanent trend toward provincial autonomy and local self-government accompanied by a hope and a vague plan that in the future the more or less independent units will recombine into the United or Federated States of China. Some who look far into the future anticipate three stages; the first being the completion of the present secessionist movement; the second the formation of northern and southern confederations respectively; the third a reunion into a single state.

To go into the detailed evidence for the existence of a definite and lasting movement of this sort would presume too much on the reader's knowledge of Chinese geography and his acquaintance with specific recent events. I shall confine myself to quite general features of the situation. The first feature is the new phase which has been assumed by the long historic antagonism of the north and the south. Roughly speaking, the revolution which established the republic and overthrew the Manchus represented a victory for the south. But the transformation during the last five years of the nominal republic into a corrupt oligarchy of satraps or military governors or feudal lords has represented a victory for the north. It is a significant fact, symbolically at least, that the most powerful remaining tuchun or military governor in China—in some respects the only powerful one who has survived the vicissitudes of the last few years—namely Chang Tso Lin, is the uncrowned king of the three Manchurian provinces. The so-called civil war of the north and south is not, however, to be understood as a conflict of republicanism located in the south and militarism in the north. Such a notion is directly contrary to facts. The "civil war" till six or eight months ago was mainly a conflict of military governors and factions, part of that struggle for personal power and wealth which has been going on all over China.

But recently events have taken a different course. In four of the southern provinces, tuchuns who seemed all powerful have toppled over, and the provinces have proclaimed or tacitly assumed their independence of both the Peking and the former military Canton governments—the province in which Canton situated being one of the four. I happened to be in Hunan, the first of the southerly provinces to get comparative independence, last fall, not long after the overthrow of the vicious despot who had ruled the province with the aid of northern troops. For a week a series of meetings were held in Changsha, the capital of the province. The burden of every speech was "Hunan for the Hunanese." The slogan embodies the spirit of two powers each aiming at becoming the central authority; it is a conflict of the principle of provincial autonomy, represented by the politically more mature south, with that of militaristic centralization, represented by Peking.

As I write, in early September (1921), the immediate issue is obscured by the fight which Wu Pei Fu is waging with the Hunanese who with nominal independence are in aim and interest allied with the south. If, as is likely, Wu Pei Fu wins, he may take one of two courses. He may use his added power to turn against Chang Tso Lin and the northern militarists which will bring him into virtual alliance with the southerners and establish him as the antagonist of the federal principle. This is the course which his earlier record would call for. Or he may yield to the usual official lust for power and money and try once more the Yuan Shi Kai policy of military centralization with himself as head, after trying out conclusions with Chang Tso Lin as his rival. This is the course which the past record of military leaders indicates. But even if Wu Pei Fu follows precedent and goes bad, he will only hasten his own final end. This is not prophecy. It is only a statement of what has uniformly happened in China just at the moment a military leader seemed to have complete power in his grasp. In other words, a victory for Wu Pei Fu may either accelerate or may retard the development of provincial autonomy according to the course he pursues. It cannot permanently prevent or deflect it.

The basic factor that makes one sure that this trend toward

local autonomy is a reality and not merely one of those meaningless shiftings of power which confuse the observer, is that it is in accord with Chinese temperament, tradition and circumstance. Feudalism is past and gone two thousand years ago, and at no period since has China possessed a working centralized government. The absolute empires which have come and gone in the last two millenniums existed by virtue of non-interference and a religious aura. The latter can never be restored; and every episode of the republic demonstrates that China with its vast and diversified territories, its population of between three hundred and fifty and four hundred million, its multitude of languages and lack of communications, its enormous local attachments sanctified by the family system and ancestral worship, cannot be managed from a single and remote centre. China rests upon a network of local and voluntary associations cemented by custom. This fact has given it its unparalleled stability and its power to progress even under the disturbed political conditions of the past ten years. I sometimes think that Americans with their own traditional contempt for politics and their spontaneous reliance upon self-help and local organization are the ones who are naturally fitted to understand China's course. The Japanese with their ingrained reliance upon the state have continually misjudged and misacted. The British understand better than we do the significance of local self-government; but they are misled by their reverence for politics so that they cannot readily find or see government when it does not take political form.

It is not too much to say that one great cause for the overthrow of the Manchus was the fact that because of the pressure of international relations they attempted to force, especially in fiscal matters, a centralization upon the provinces wholly foreign to the spirit of the people. This created hostility where before there had been indifference. China may possibly not emerge from her troubles a unified nation, any more than a much smaller and less populous Europe emerged from the break-up of the Holy Roman Empire, a single state. Indeed one often wonders, not that China is divided, but that she is not much more broken up than she is. But one thing is certain. Whatever progress China finally succeeds in making will come from a variety of local centres, not from Peking or Canton. It will be effected by means of associations and organizations which even though they assume a political form are not primarily political in nature.

Criticisms are passed, especially by foreigners, upon the present trend of events. The criticisms are more than plausible. It is evident that the present weakness of China is due to her divided condition. Hence it is natural to argue that the present movement being one of secession and general disintegration will increase the weakness of the country. It is also evident that many of China's troubles are due to the absence of any efficient administrative system; it is reasonable to argue that China cannot get even railways and universal education without a strong and stable central government. There is no doubt about the facts. It is not surprising that many friends of China deeply deplore the present tendency while some regard it as the final accomplishment of the long predicted breakup of China. But remedies for China's ills based upon ignoring history, psychology and actual conditions are so utopian that it is not worth while to argue whether or not they are theoretically desirable. The remedy of China's troubles by a strong, centralized government is on a par with curing disease by the expulsion of a devil. The evil of sectionalism is real, but since it is real it cannot be dealt with by trying a method which implies its non-existence. If the devil is really there, he will not be exorcized by a formula. If the trouble is internal, not due to an external demon, the disease can be cured only by using the factors of health and vigor which the patient already possesses. And in China while these factors of recuperation and growth are numerous, they all exist in connection with local organizations and voluntary associations. The increasing volume of the cry that the "tuchuns must go" comes from the provincial and local interests which have been insulted and violated by a nominally centralized but actually chaotic situation. After this negative work is completed, the constructive rebuilding of China can proceed only by utilizing local interests and abilities. In China the movement will be the opposite of that which occurred in Japan. It will be from the periphery to the centre.

Another objection to the present tendency has force especially from the foreign standpoint. As already stated, the efforts of the Manchu dynasty in its latter days to enhance central power were due to international pressure. Foreign nations treated Peking as if it were a capital like London, Paris or Berlin, and in its efforts to meet foreign demands it had to try to become such a centre. The result was disaster. But foreign nations still want to have a single centre which may be held responsible. And subconsciously, if not consciously, this desire is responsible for much of the objection of foreign nationals to the local autonomy movement. They well know that it is going to take a long time to realize the ideal of federation, and meantime where and what is to be the agency responsible for diplomatic relations, the enforcing of indemnities and the securing of concessions?

In one respect the secessionist tendency is dangerous to China herself as well as inconvenient to the powers. It will readily stimulate the desire and ability of foreign nations to interfere in China's domestic affairs. There will be many centres at which to carry on intrigues and from which to get concessions instead of one or two. There is also danger that one foreign nation may line up with one group of provinces, and another foreign nation with another group, so that international friction will increase. Even now some Japanese sources and even such an independent liberal paper as Robert Young's Japan Chronicle are starting or reporting the rumor that the Cantonese experiment is supported by subsidies supplied by American capitalists in the hope of economic concessions. The rumor was invented for a sinister purpose. But it illustrates the sort of situation that may come into existence if there are several political centres in China and one foreign nation backs one and another nation, another.

The danger is real enough. But it cannot be dealt with by attempting the impossible—namely checking the movement toward local autonomy, even though disintegration may temporarily accompany it. The danger only emphasizes the fundamental fact of the whole Chinese situation; that its essence is time. The evils and troubles of China are real enough, and there is no blinking the fact that they are largely of her own making, due to corruption, inefficiency and absence of popular education. But no one who knows the common people doubts that they will win through if they are given time. And in the concrete this means that they be left politically alone to work out their own destiny. There will doubtless be proposals at the Pacific Conference to place China under some kind of international tutelage. This chapter and the events connected with the tendency which it reports will be cited as showing this need. Some of the schemes will spring from motives that are hostile to China. Some will be benevolently conceived in a desire to save China from herself and shorten her period of chaos and confusion. But the hope of the world's peace, as well as of China's freedom, lies in adhering to a policy of Hands Off. Give China a chance. Give her time. The danger lies in being in a hurry, in impatience, possibly in the desire of America to show that we are a power in international affairs and that we too have a positive foreign policy. And a benevolent policy of supporting China from without, instead of promoting her aspirations from within, may in the end do China about as much harm as a policy conceived in malevolence.

[July, 1921.]

VII

A PARTING OF THE WAYS FOR AMERICA

1

The realities of American policy in China and toward China are going to be more seriously tested in the future than they ever have been in the past. Japanese papers have been full of protests against any attempt by the Pacific Conference to place Japan on trial. Would that American journals were full of warnings that America is on trial at the Conference as to the sincerity and intelligent goodwill behind her amiable professions. The world will not stop with the Pacific Conference; the latter, however important, will not arrest future developments, and the United States will continue to be on trial till she has established by her acts a permanent and definite attitude. For the realities of the situation cannot be exhausted in any formula or in any set of diplomatic agreements, even if the Conference confounds the fears of pessimists and results in a harmonious union of the powers in support of China's legitimate aspirations for free political and economic growth.

The Conference, however, stands as a symbol of the larger situation; and its decisions or lack of them will be a considerable factor in the determination of subsequent events. Sometimes one is obliged to fall back on a trite phrase. We are genuinely at a parting of the ways. Even if we should follow in our old path, there would none the less be a parting of the ways, for we cannot consistently tread the old path unless we are animated by a much more conscious purpose and a more general and intelligent knowledge of affairs than have controlled our activities in the past.

The ideas expressed by an English correspondent about the fear that America is soon to be an active source of danger in the Far East are not confined to persons on foreign shores. The prevailing attitude in some circles of American opinion is that called by President Hibben cynical pessimism. All professed radicals and many liberals believe that if our course has been better in the past it has been due to geographical accidents combined with indifference and with our undeveloped economic status. Consequently they believe that since we have now become what is called a world-power and a nation which exports instead of importing capital, our course will soon be as bad as that of any of the rest of them. In some quarters this opinion is clearly an emotional reaction following the disillusionments of Versailles. In others, it is due to adherence to a formula: nothing in international affairs can come out of capitalism and America is emphatically a capitalistic country. Whether or not these feelings are correct, they are not discussable; neither an emotion nor an absolute formula is subject to analysis.

But there are specific elements in the situation which give grounds for apprehension as to the future. These specific elements are capable of detection and analysis. An adequate realization of their nature will be a large factor in preventing cynical apprehensions from becoming actual. This chapter is an attempt at a preliminary listing, inadequate, of course, as any preliminary examination must be. While an a priori argument based on a fatalistic formula as to how a "capitalistic nation" must conduct itself does not appeal to me, there are nevertheless concrete facts which are suggested by that formula. Part of our comparatively better course in China in the past is due to the fact that we have not had the continuous and close alliance between the State Department and big banking interests which is found in the case of foreign powers. No honest well-informed history of developments in China could be written in which the Russian Asiatic Bank, the Foreign Bank of Belgium, the French Indo-China Bank and Banque Industrielle, the Yokohama Specie Bank, the Hongkong-Shanghai Bank, etc., did not figure prominently. These banks work in the closest harmony, not only with railway and construction syndicates and big manufacturing interests at home, but also with their respective foreign offices. It is hardly too much to say that legations and banks have been in most important matters the right and left hands of the same body. American business interests have complained an the past that the American government does not give to American traders abroad the same support that the nationals of other states receive. In the past these complaints have centred largely about actual wrongs suffered or believed to have been suffered by American business undertakings carried on in a foreign country. With the present expansion of capital and of commerce, the same complaints and demands are going to be made not with reference to grievances suffered, but with reference to furthering, to pushing American commercial interests in connection with large banking groups. It would take a credulous person to deny the influence of big business in domestic politics. As we become more interested in commerce and banking enterprises what assurance have we that the alliance will not be transferred to international politics?

It should be noted that the policy of the open door as affirmed by the great powers—and as frequently violated by them—even if it be henceforth observed in good faith, does not adequately protect us from this danger. The open door policy is not primarily a policy about China herself but rather about the policies of foreign powers toward one another with respect to China. It demands equality of economic opportunity for different nations. Were it enforced, it would prevent the granting of monopolies to any one nation: there is nothing in it to render impossible a conjoint exploitation of China by foreign powers, an organized monopoly in which each nation has its due share with respect to others. Such an organization might conceivably reduce friction among the great powers, and thereby reduce the danger of future wars—as long as China herself is impotent to go to war. The agreement might conceivably for a considerable time be of benefit to China herself. But it is clear that for the United States to become a partner in any such arrangement would involve a reversal of our historic policy in the Far East. It might be technically consistent with the open door policy, but it would be a violation of the larger sense in which the American people has understood and praised that ideal. He is blind who does not see that there are forces making for such a reversal. And since we are all more or less blind, an opening of our eyes to the danger is one of the conditions of its not being realized.

One of the forces which is operative is indicated by the phrase that an international agreement on an economic and financial basis might be of value to China herself. The mere suggestion that such a thing is possible is abhorrent to many, especially to radicals. There seems to be something sinister in it. So it is worth explaining how and why it might be so. In the first place, it would obviously terminate the particularistic grabbing for "leased" territory, concessions and spheres of influence which has so damaged China. At the present time, the point of this remark lies in its implied reference to Japan, as at one time it might have applied to Russia. Fear of Japan's aims in China is not confined to China; the fear is widespread. An international economic arrangement may therefore be plausibly presented as the easiest and most direct method of relieving China of the Japanese menace. For Japan to stay out would be to give herself away; if she came in, it would subject Japanese activities to constant scrutiny and control. There is no doubt that part of the fear of Japan regarding the Pacific Conference is due to a belief that some such arrangement is contemplated. The case is easily capable of such presentation as to make it appeal to Americans who are really friendly to China and who haven't the remotest interest in her economic exploitation.

The arrangement would, for example, automatically eliminate the Lansing-Ishii agreement with its embarrassing ambiguous recognition of Japan's *special* interests in China.

The other factor is domestic. The distraction and civil wars of China are commonplaces. So is the power exercised by the military governors and generals. The greater one's knowledge, the more one perceives how intimately the former evil is dependent upon the latter. The financial plight of the Chinese government, its continual foreign borrowings which threaten bankruptcy in the near future, depend upon militaristic domination and wild expenditure for unproductive purposes and squeeze. Without this expense, China would have no great difficulty henceforth in maintaining a balance in her budget. The retardation of public education whose advancement—especially in elementary schools—is China's greatest single need is due to the same cause. So is the growth in official corruption which is rapidly extending into business and private life.

In fact, every one of the obstacles to the progress of China is connected with the rule of military factions and their struggles with one another for complete mastery. An economic international agreement among the great powers can be made which would surely reduce and possibly eliminate the greatest evils of "militarism." Many liberal Chinese say in private that they would be willing to have a temporary international receivership for government finance, provided they could be assured of its nature and the exact date and conditions of its termination—a proviso which they are sensible enough to recognize would be extremely difficult of attainment. American leadership in forming and executing any such scheme would, they feel, afford the best reassurance as to its nature and terms. Under such circumstances a plausible case can be made out for proposals which, under the guise of traditional American friendship for China, would in fact commit us to a reversal of our historic policy.

There are radicals abroad and at home who think that our entrance into a Consortium already proves that we have entered upon the road of reversal and who naturally see in the Pacific Conference the next logical step. I have previously stated my own belief that our State Department proposed the Consortium primarily for political ends, as a means of checking the policy pursued by Japan of making unproductive loans to China in return for which she was getting an immediate grip on China's natural resources and preparing the way for direct administrative and financial control when the day of reckoning and foreclosure should finally come. I also said that the Consortium was between two stools, the financial and the political and that up to the present its chief value had been negative and preventive, and that jealousy or lack of interest by Japan and Great Britain in any constructive policy on the part of the Consortium was likely to maintain the same condition. I have seen no reason thus far to change my mind on this point, nor in regard to the further belief that probably the interests of China in the end will be best served by the continuation of this deterrent function. But the question is bound to arise: why continue the Consortium if it isn't doing anything? The pressure of foreign powers interested in the exploitation of China and of impatient American economic interests may combine to put an end to the present rather otiose existence led by the Consortium. The two stools between which the past action of the American government has managed to swing the Consortium may be united to form a single solid bench.

At the risk of being charged with credulous gullibility, or something worse, I add that up to the present time the American phase of the Consortium hasn't shown perceptible signs of becoming a club exercised by American finance over China's economic integrity and independence. I believe the repeated statements of the American representative that he himself and the interests he represents would be glad if China proved her ability to finance her own public utilities without resorting to foreign loans. This belief is confirmed by the first public utterance of the new American minister to China who in his reference to the Consortium laid emphasis upon its deterrent function and upon the stimulation it has given to Chinese bankers to finance public utilities. And it is the merest justice to Mr. Stevens, the American representative, to say that he represents the conservative investment type of banker, not the "promotion" type, and that thus far his great concern has been the problem of protecting the buyer of such securities as are passed on by the banks to the ultimate investor—so much so that he has aroused criticism from American business interests impatient for speedy action. But there is a larger phase of the Consortium concerning which I think apprehensions may reasonably be entertained.

Suppose, if merely by way of hypothesis, that the American government is genuinely interested in China and in making the policy of the open door and Chinese territorial and administrative integrity a reality, not merely a name, and suppose that it is interested in doing so from an American self-interest sufficiently enlightened to perceive that the political and economic advancement of the United States is best furthered by a policy which is identical with China's ability to develop herself freely and independently: what then would be the wise American course? In short, it would be to view our existing European interests and issues (due to the war) and our Far Eastern interests and issues as parts of one and the same problem. If we are actuated by the motive hypothetically imputed to our government and we fail in its realization, the chief reason will be that we regard the European question and the Asiatic problem as two different questions, or because we identify them from the wrong end.

Our present financial interest in Europe is enormous. It involves not merely foreign governmental loans but a multitude of private advances and commitments. These financial entanglements affect not merely our industry and commerce but our politics. They involve much more immediately pressing concerns than to our Asiatic relations, and they involve billions where the latter involve millions. The danger under such conditions that our Asiatic relations will be sacrificed to our European is hardly fanciful.

To make this abstract statement concrete, the firm of bankers, J. P. Morgan & Co., which is most heavily involved in European indebtedness to the United States, is the firm which is the leading spirit in the Consortium for China. It seems almost inevitable that the Asiatic problem should look like small potatoes in comparison with the European one, especially as our own industrial recuperation is so closely connected with European relations, while the Far East cuts a negligible figure. To my mind the real danger to set out upon selfish exploitation of China: intelligent self-interest, tradition and the fact that our chief asset in China is our past freedom from a predatory course, dictate a course of cooperation with China. The danger is that China will be subordinated and sacrificed because of primary preoccupation with the high finance and politics of Europe, that she will be lost in the shuffle.

The European aspect of the problem can be made more concrete by reference to Great Britain in particular. That country suffers from the embarrassment of the Japanese alliance. She has already made it sufficiently clear that she would like to draw America into the alliance, making it tripartite, since that would be the easiest way of maintaining good relations with both Japan and the United States. There is no likelihood that any such step will be consummated. But British diplomacy is experienced and astute. And by force of circumstances our high finance has contracted a sort of economic alliance with Great Britain. There is no wish to claim superior virtue for America or to appeal to the strong current of anti-British sentiment. But the British foreign office exists and operates apart from the tradition of liberalism which has mainly actuated English domestic politics. It stands peculiarly for the *Empire* side of the British Empire, no matter what party is in the saddle in domestic affairs. Every resource will be employed to bring about a settlement at the Pacific Conference which, even though it includes some degree of compromise on the part of Great Britain, will bend the Asiatic policy of the United States to the British traditions in the Far East, instead of committing Great Britain to combining with the United States in making a reality of the integrity of China to which both countries are nominally committed. It does not seem an extreme statement to say that the immediate issues of the Conference depend upon the way in which our financial commitments in Europe are treated, either as reasons for our making concessions to European policy or on the other hand as a means of securing an adherence of the European powers to the traditional American policy.

A publicist in China who is of British origin and a sincere friend of China remarked in private conversation that if the United States could not secure the adherence of Great Britain to her Asiatic policy by persuasion (he was deploring the Japanese alliance) she might do so by buying it—through remission of her national debt to us. It is not necessary to resort to the measure so baldly suggested. But the remark at least suggests that our involvement in European, especially British, finance and politics may be treated in either of two ways for either of two results.

2

That the Chinese people generally speaking has a less antagonistic feeling toward the United States than towards other powers seems to me an undoubted fact. The feeling has been disturbed at divers times by the treatment of the Chinese upon the Pacific coast, by the exclusion act, by the turning over of our interest in the building of the Peking-Canton (or Hankow) railway to a European group, by the Lansing-Ishii agreement, and finally by the part played by President Wilson in the Versailles decision regarding Shantung. Those disturbances in the main, however, have made them dubious as to our skill, energy and intelligence rather than as to our good-will. Americans, taken individually and collectively, are to the Chinese—at least such was my impression—a rather simple folk, taking the word in its good and its deprecatory sense. In noting the Chinese reaction to the proposed Pacific Conference, it was interesting to see the combination of an almost unlimited hope that the United States was to lead in protecting them from further aggressions and in rectifying existing evils, with a lack of confidence, a fear that the United States would have something put over on it.

Friendly feeling is of course mainly based upon a negative fact, the fact that the United States has taken no part in "leasing" territories, establishing spheres and setting up extra-national post-offices. On the positive side stands the contribution made by Americans to education, especially medical, and that of girls and women, and to philanthropy and relief. Politically, there are the early service of Burlinghame, the open door policy of John Hay (though failure to maintain it in fact while securing signatures to it on paper is a considerable part of the Chinese belief in our defective energy) and the part played by the United States in moderating the terms of the settlement of the Boxer outbreak, in addition to a considerable number of minor helpful acts. China also remembers that we were the only nation to take exception to the treaties embodying the Twenty-one Demands. While our exception was chiefly made on the basis of our own interests which these treaties might injuriously affect, a sentiment exists that the protest was a pledge of assistance to China when the time should be opportune for raising the whole question. And without doubt the reservation made on May 16, 1915, by our State Department is a strong card at the forthcoming Conference if the Department wishes to play it.

From an American standpoint, the open door principle represents one of the only two established principles of American diplomacy, the other being, of course, the Monroe Doctrine. In connection with sentimental or idealistic associations which have clustered about it, it constitutes us in some vague fashion in both the Chinese and American public opinion a sort of guardian or at least spokesman of the interests of China in relation to foreign powers. Although, as was pointed out in a former chapter, the open door policy directly concerns other nations in their relation to China rather than China herself, yet the violation of the policy by other powers has been so frequent and so much to the detriment of China, that American interest, prestige and moral sentiment are now implicated in such an enforcement of it as will redound to the advantage of China.

Citizens of other countries are often irritated by a suggestion of such a relationship between the United States and China. It presents itself as a proclamation of superior national virtue under cover of which the United States aims to establish its influence in China at the expense of other countries. The irritation is exasperated by the fact that the situation as it stands is an undoubted economic and political asset of the United States in China. We may concede without argument any contention that the situation is not due to any superior virtue but rather to contingencies of history and geography—in which respect it is not unlike many things that pass for virtues with individuals. The contention may be admitted without controversy because it is not pertinent to the main issue. The question is not so much how the state of affairs came about as what it now is, how it is to be treated and what consequences are in flow from it. It is a fact that up to the present an intelligent self-interest of America has coincided with the interests of a stable, independent and progressive China. It is also a fact that American traditions and sentiments have gathered about this consideration so that now there is widespread conviction in the American people of moral obligations of assistance and friendly protection owed by us to China. At present, no policy can be entered upon that does not bear the semblance of fairness and goodwill. We have at least so much protection against the dangers discussed in the prior chapter.

Among Americans in China and presumably at home there is a strong feeling that we should adopt for the future stronger and more positive policies than we have maintained in the past. This feeling seems to me fraught with dangers unless we make very clear to ourselves in just what respects we are to continue and make good in a more positive manner our traditional policy. To some extent our past policy has been one of drifting. Radical change in this respect may go further than appears upon the surface in altering other fundamental aspects of our policy. What is condemned as drifting is in effect largely the same thing that is also praised as non-interference. A detailed settled policy, no matter how "constructive" it may appear to be, can hardly help involving us in the domestic policies of China, an affair of factions and a game which the Chinese understand and play much better than any foreigners. Such an involvement would at once lessen a present large asset in China, aloofness from internal intrigues and struggles.

The specific protests of Chinese in this country—mainly Cantonese—against the Consortium seem to me mainly based on misapprehension. But their *general* attitude of opposition nevertheless conveys an important lesson. It is based on a belief that the effect of the Consortium will be to give the Peking government a factitious advantage in the internal conflict which is waging in China, so that to all intents and purposes it will mark a taking of sides on our part. It is well remembered that the effect of the "reorganization" loan of the prior Consortium—in which the United States was *not* a partner—was to give Yuan Shi Kai the funds which seated him and the militarist faction after him, firmly in the governmental saddle. Viewing the matter from a larger point of view than that of Canton vs. Peking, the most fundamental objection I heard brought by Chinese against the Consortium was in effect as follows: The republican revolution in China has still to be wrought out; the beginning of ten years ago has been arrested. It remains to fight it out. The inevitable effect of increased foreign financial and economic interest in China, even admitting that its industrial effect was advantageous to China, would be to create an interest in *stabilizing* China politically, which in effect would mean to sanctify the status quo, and prevent the development of a revolution which cannot be accomplished without internal disorders that would affect foreign investments unfavorably. These considerations are not mentioned for the sake of throwing light on the Consortium: they are cited as an illustration of the probability that a too positive and constructive development of our tradition of goodwill to China would involve us in an interference with Chinese domestic affairs injurious to China's welfare, to that free and independent development in which we profess such interest.

But how, it will be asked, are we to protect China from foreign depredations, particularly those of Japan, how are we to change our nominal goodwill into a reality, if we do not enter much more positive and detailed policies? If there was in existence at the present time any such thing as a diplomacy of peoples as distinct from a diplomacy of governments, the question would mean something quite different from what it now means. As things now stand the people should profoundly *distrust* the politicians' love for China. It is too frequently the reverse side of fear and incipient hatred of Japan, colored perhaps by anti-British feeling.

There should be no disguising of the situation. The aggressive activities of other nations in China, centering but not exhausted at this time in Japan, are not merely sources of trouble to China but they are potential causes of trouble in our own international relationships. We are committed by our tradition and by the present actualities of the situation to attempting something positive for China as respects her international status, to live up to our responsibility is a most difficult and delicate matter. We have on the one side to avoid getting entangled in quasi-imperialistic European policies in Asia, whether under the guise of altruism, of putting ourselves in a position where we can exercise a more effective supervision of their behavior, or by means of economic expansion. On the other side, we have to avoid drifting into that kind of covert or avowed antagonism to European and Japanese imperialism which will only increase friction, encourage a combination especially of Great Britain and Japan—-or of France and Japan—against us, and bring war appreciably nearer.

We need to bear in mind that China will not be saved from outside herself. Even if by a successful war we should relieve China from Japanese encroachments, from all encroachments, China would not of necessity be brought nearer her legitimate goal of orderly and prosperous internal development. Apart from the question of how far war can now settle any fundamental issues without begetting others as dangerous, China of all countries is the one where settlement by force, especially by outside force, is least applicable, and most likely to be enormously disserviceable. China is used to taking time to deal with her problems: she can neither understand not profit by impatient methods of the western world which are profoundly alien to her genius. Moreover a civilization which is on a continental scale, which is so old that the rest of us are parvenus in comparison, which is thick and closely woven, cannot be hurried in its development without disaster. Transformation from within is its sole way out, and we can best help China by trying to see to it that she gets the time she needs in order to effect this transformation, whether or not we like the particular form it assumes at any particular time.

A successful war in behalf of China would leave untouched her problems of education, of factional and sectional forces, of political immaturity showing itself in present incapacity for organization. It would affect her industrial growth undoubtedly, but in all human probability for the worse, increasing the likelihood that she would enter upon an industrialization which would repeat the worst evils of western industrial life, without the immunities, resistances and remedial measures which the West has evolved. The imagination cannot conceive a worse crime than fastening western industrialism upon China before she has developed within herself the meaning of coping with the forces which it would release. The danger is great enough as it is. War waged in China's behalf by western powers and western methods would make the danger practically irresistible. In addition we should gain a permanent interest in China which is likely to be of the most dangerous character to ourselves. If we were not committed by it to future imperialism, we should be luckier than we have any right to hope to be. These things are said against a mental protest to admitting even by implication the prospect of war with Japan, but it seems necessary to say them.

These remarks are negative and vague as to our future course. They imply a confession of lack of such wisdom as would enable me to make positive definite proposals. But at least I have confidence in the wisdom and goodwill of the American and other peoples to deal with the problem, if they are only called into action. And the first condition of calling wisdom and goodwill into effective existence is to recognize the seriousness of the problem and the utter futility of trying to force its solution by impatient and hurried methods. Pro-Japanese apologetics is dangerous; it obscures the realities of the situation. An irritated anti-Japanism that would hasten the solution of the Chinese problem merely by attacking Japan is equally fatal to discovering and applying a proper method.

More specifically and also more generically, proper publicity is the greatest need. If, as Secretary Hughes has intimated, a settlement of the problems of the Pacific is made a condition of arriving at an agreement regarding reduction and limitation of armaments, it is likely that the Conference might better never be held. In eagerness to do something which will pass as a settlement, either China's—and Siberia's—interests will be sacrificed in some unfair compromise, or irritation and friction will be increased—and in the end so will armaments. In any literal sense, it is ridiculous to suppose that the problems of the Pacific can be settled in a few weeks, or months—or years. Yet the discussion of the problems, in separation from the question of armament, may be of great use. For it may further that publicity which is a pre-condition of any genuine settlement. This involves the public in diplomacy. But it also involves a wider publicity, one which will enlighten the world about the facts of Asia, internal and international.

Scepticism about Foreign Offices, as they are at present conducted, is justified. But scepticism about the power of public opinion, if it can be aroused and instructed, to reshape Foreign Office policies means hopelessness about the future of the world. Let everything possible be done to reduce armament, if only to secure a naval holiday on the part of the three great naval powers, and if only for the sake of lessening taxation. Let the Conference on Problems devote itself to discussing and making known as fully and widely as possible the element and scope of those problems, and the fears—or should one call them hopes?—of the cynics will be frustrated. It is not so important that a decision in the American sense of the Yap question be finally and forever arrived at, as it is that the need of China and the Orient in general for freer and fuller communications with the rest of the world be made clear—and so on, down or up the list of agenda. The commercial open door is needed. But the need is greater that the door be opened to light, to knowledge and understanding. If these forces will not create a public opinion which will in time secure a lasting and just settlement of other problems, there is no recourse save despair of civilization. Liberals can do something better than predicting failure and impugning motives. They can work for the opened door of open diplomacy, of continuous and intelligent inquiry, of discussion free from propaganda. To shirk this responsibility on the alleged ground that economic imperialism and organized greed will surely bring the Conference to failure is supine and snobbish. It is one of the factors that may lead the United States to take the wrong course in the parting of the ways.

[October, 1921.]